T0329175

Cambridge Elements ☰

Elements in Ethics
edited by
Ben Eggleston
University of Kansas
Dale E. Miller
Old Dominion University, Virginia

THOMAS REID ON THE ETHICAL LIFE

Terence Cuneo
University of Vermont

CAMBRIDGE
UNIVERSITY PRESS

CAMBRIDGE
UNIVERSITY PRESS

University Printing House, Cambridge CB2 8BS, United Kingdom

One Liberty Plaza, 20th Floor, New York, NY 10006, USA

477 Williamstown Road, Port Melbourne, VIC 3207, Australia

314–321, 3rd Floor, Plot 3, Splendor Forum, Jasola District Centre,
New Delhi – 110025, India

79 Anson Road, #06–04/06, Singapore 079906

Cambridge University Press is part of the University of Cambridge.

It furthers the University's mission by disseminating knowledge in the pursuit of
education, learning, and research at the highest international levels of excellence.

www.cambridge.org
Information on this title: www.cambridge.org/9781108706896
DOI: 10.1017/9781108756563

First published 2020

A catalogue record for this publication is available from the British Library.

ISBN 978-1-108-70689-6 Paperback
ISSN 2516-4031 (online)
ISSN 2516-4023 (print)

Thomas Reid on the Ethical Life

Elements in Ethics

DOI: 10.1017/9781108756563
First published online: August 2020

Terence Cuneo
University of Vermont
Author for correspondence: Terence Cuneo, tcuneo@uvm.edu

Abstract: This Element presents the rudiments of Thomas Reid's agency-centered ethical theory. According to this theory, an ethical theory must address three primary questions. What is it to be an agent? What is ethical reality like, such that agents could know it? And how can agents respond to ethical reality, commit themselves to being regulated by it, and act well in doing so? Reid's answers to these questions is wide-ranging, borrowing from the rational intuitionist, sentimentalist, Aristotelian, and Protestant natural law traditions. This Element explores how Reid blends together these influences, how he might respond to concerns raised by rival traditions, and specifies what distinguishes his approach from those of other modern philosophers.

Keywords: Ethics, agency, action, Reid, modernity

ISBNs: 9781108706896 (PB), 9781108756563 (OC)
ISSNs: 2516-4031 (online), 2516-4023 (print)

In memory of my friend and first philosophical companion,

E. George Lundstedt,

(1969–2018)

with whom I first read Reid.

Memory Eternal.

Contents

Introduction

My project in this short book is to present the rudiments of (what I call) Thomas Reid's agency-centered ethical theory. In doing so, my aim is not to offer a comprehensive overview of Reid's position, break new conceptual ground, or present a strikingly novel interpretation of Reid's views. It is rather to identify Reid's leading questions and why he answers them as he does.

There would be little reason to write a similar book on Hume's ethical theory or Kant's. Their views have already been the subject of both extensive critical commentary and exegetical controversy. The work in these areas of scholarship primarily consists in fine-tuning, correcting, and weighing the relative merits of the different available interpretations. In contrast, there is excellent reason to write a book whose primary aim is to identify Reid's leading questions and how he answers them. For despite having exercised considerable influence, Reid's views in ethics are unfamiliar to most philosophers today. (Throughout this discussion, I use the term "ethics" broadly to concern how we should live; it needn't pertain to morality more narrowly understood.) And to the extent Reid's views are familiar, many seem to think of Reid as a rational intuitionist in the mold of Samuel Clarke and Richard Price.[1] While Reid's rationalist tendencies run deep, I will be developing an interpretation according to which Reid's leading questions are rather different from those of the rational intuitionists.

The interpretation is one that emphasizes the synthetic character of Reid's approach, which fuses insights from the rational intuitionist, sentimentalist, Protestant natural law, and Stoic traditions. (I will have more to say about the representatives of and the views defended in these traditions later.) Speaking autobiographically, if I have experienced any shift in my own take on Reid's views over the last twenty years, it is that when placed against the backdrop of the history of modernity, they look more distinctive than they once did. Reid's questions, the answers he offers to them, and the theoretical framework he employs seem not to enjoy close parallels among his interlocutors. I am tempted to say that this is largely because the general position Reid develops is highly eclectic. Reid seemed comfortable borrowing and blending together whatever views seemed best to him, regardless of their pedigree. In my judgment, it is this approach to ethical theorizing—and the views that emerge from Reid's imple-mentation of it—that make Reid a particularly interesting figure with whom to engage.

Reid embraces what I have called an agency-centered approach to ethical theorizing. By an *agency-centered* approach, I mean one according to which agency intersects with the subject matter of ethics in a sufficiently wide range of

---

[1] See MacIntyre (1966, 177) and Rawls (2000, 9).

important ways that we cannot satisfactorily engage in ethical theorizing without committing ourselves to, and ultimately developing, particular understandings of agency. Under an agency-centered account, the way to approach ethical theorizing is not to begin as the rational intuitionists did by defending the "eternal and immutable" character of moral obligation. Nor is it to begin, as the sentimentalists did by identifying what in fact moves our approbation or disapprobation. Nor is it to begin as G. E. Moore did by examining the character of moral concepts or language, say, by asking what the term "good" means. Instead, the way to theorize is to start by asking what ethical reality must be like if we can respond to it, commit ourselves to being regulated by it, and act well in doing so. And it is to begin by asking what agency must be like if we are to make sense of ascriptions of moral accountability and the character of the reactive attitudes, such as resentment and gratitude, which themselves often track ethical reality. This book explores different dimensions of Reid's agency-centered approach.

I can offer here a taste of what renders Reid's agency-centered approach distinctive. Reid devotes not quite half of the *Essays on the Active Powers of Man* (1788) to offering a detailed taxonomy of the contributors to action, or what he calls "motives." According to Reid's taxonomy, there are three types of motives. There are, first, the *mechanical motives*, which incorporate both "blind impulses" (such as the instinct to sleep) and "habits" (such as those operative in pronouncing sounds in certain ways when we speak) (EAP III.i). There are, second, the *animal motives*, which include what Reid calls the benevolent and malevolent affections, passions, dispositions, and opinions (EAP III.ii). These include attitudes such as gratitude, pity, and compassion. Finally, there are what he calls the two *rational principles of action*, our good on the whole and duty.

I will have much more to say about motives, especially the two rational principles of action. For present purposes, suffice it to say that one finds in the rational intuitionists and the Protestant natural law (or deontological) tradition little interest in motives or moral psychology. Given the rational intuitionists' nearly exclusive interest in defending the robust objectivity of the fundamental moral principles, this is understandable. And given the Protestant natural law (or deontological) tradition's efforts to distance itself from Aristotelian virtue-centered approaches, which emphasize the role of motives, it is unsurprising that members of this tradition barely discuss related issues.[2] In contrast, Reid's interest in moral psychology runs deep.

---

[2] Heydt (2018, 24) marks a dramatic shift in interest in the passions, comparing scholastic textbooks in moral philosophy with those written by Protestant natural law (deontological) theorists such as Carmichael. The scholastics devoted extensive attention to the passions in

There appear to be two primary explanations why. The first more or less falls out of Reid's commitment to an agency-centered approach to ethical theorizing. This approach is predicated on the conviction that any satisfactory approach to ethical theorizing must be located within an account of what it is to be an agent. It places questions such as the following at the heart of ethical theorizing: What would it take for us to be capable of exercising effective agency, especially the sort that can support ascriptions of responsibility? Reid's answer is (in part) that we must act from motives. For without motives, what Reid calls active power (our executive practical capacity) would be "given us in vain. Having no motive to direct our active exertions, the mind would, in all cases, be in a state of perfect indifference, to do this or that, or nothing at all" (EAP III.i.i: 74).

Add now that while motives are a necessary condition of exercising agency, they can push (or pull) us in a variety of incompatible directions, fracturing and undercutting agency. To avoid such conflicts, we need to manage our motives. Reid often gives the impression that such management consists in keeping the various mechanical and animal motives in check (EAP III.iii.ii). But his considered view is that such self-management involves much more than this. It also involves cultivating certain dispositions. When discussing the benevolent affections, which are a species of the animal principles of action, Reid writes that we are "social creatures, whose happiness or misery is very much connected with that of our fellow men" (EAP III.iii.iii: 164). Because of this, "a regard to our own good ought to lead us to cultivate and exercise" the benevolent affections, "as every benevolent affection makes the good of others to be our own" (EAP III.iii.iii: 164). A second explanation, then, for why Reid pays so much attention to motives is that doing so enables him to illustrate how agents can engage in effective rational agency, which is a topic of central importance to agency-centered approaches.

As I say, the foregoing offers just a taste of what is distinctive about Reid's agency-centered approach. One finds the fuller offering in the subsequent discussion. I have divided this discussion into four segments. The first section, "Normative Governance," introduces Reid's agency-centered understanding of ethics. As its title indicates, the section explores the topic of how, according to Reid, we are to govern our tendencies and behavior. One could think of this section as treating that dimension of agency-centered approaches that concerns so-called normative ethics. The second section, "Action, Motives, Power," explores some ambiguities in and puzzling features of Reid's understanding of these components of agency, advancing several interpretations of what Reid

---

their textbooks. In contrast, Heydt notes that in "Carmichael's commentary on Pufendorf's compendium, discussion of the passions takes up *three pages*. . . . In Pufendorf's works on natural law, the passions are barely mentioned." *Cp.* Radcliffe (2018, appendix).

is saying. This section concerns that dimension of agency-centered approaches that intersects with action theory. The third section, "Two Challenges," brings Reid's view into conversation with both the Aristotelian-Thomistic and sentimentalist traditions by identifying resources available to Reid in order to answer their central worries about his project. This section explores that dimension of agency-centered approaches that concerns metaethics. The brief concluding section, "The Sidgwickean Characterization," introduces Sidgwick's claim that a deep divide marks the ancients' approach to ethical theorizing from that of the moderns. I ask whether Reid clearly falls on the moderns' side of Sidgwick's divide, claiming that he does not. Reid's place in the history of modernity is distinctive.

Because my primary aim is to articulate the main lines of Reid's answers to his leading questions in the *Essays on the Active Powers of Man*, there are a variety of topics that Reid addresses that I do not. And among the issues I do treat, all of them deserve to be explored in greater detail. Moreover, there are historical influences on and parallels to Reid's views of which I do not take note.[3] Finally, I have not attempted to explore the various ways in which Reid's positions anticipate well-known contemporary views such as W. D. Ross's deontological pluralism and Derek Parfit's "non-metaphysical cognitivism."[4] Still, if this book achieves its purpose, it will have articulated an interpretation of Reid that takes us to the core of his project. That core consists in a set of claims that lie at the intersection of ethics and the philosophy of action. Having these claims clearly articulated should position others not only to familiarize themselves with Reid's position but also to correct and fine-tune the interpretation offered here.

Let me close by saying a word about those for whom I have written this book. It is written for two primary audiences: those who may have had some exposure to Reid's thought but know little about his ethical theory, and those who know something about ethical theory and its history but know little about Reid's contribution to it. My hope regarding the first group of philosophers is that they will find this discussion enriches their understanding of Reid, opening up further avenues of investigation. My hope regarding the second group of philosophers is that they will find in Reid's ethical theorizing a set of commitments that connects in unusual and illuminating ways with the work of the ancients and contemporary philosophers. I realize that there are many with an interest or background in philosophy who fall into neither of these two groups.

---

[3] Those interested in the figures and sources that influenced Reid's ethical theorizing should consult Haakonssen (2007, Introduction) and Heydt (2018).

[4] Ross (1930/2007) and Parfit (2011, ch. 31).

While they are not my primary audience, I hope that they, too, will benefit from engaging with this interpretation of Reid's ethical theory.

***

I'd like to thank Bill Davis, Esther Kroeker, Nick Wolterstorff, Todd Buras along with the members of a graduate seminar he led at Baylor University, and the University of Vermont Ethics Group of Sin yee Chan, Tyler Doggett, Randall Harp, and Kate Nolfi, for their feedback on the material here. Among the UVM philosophers, Doggett was kind enough to give me written comments on a draft of the manuscript. I'd also like to thank my colleague Randall Harp for helping me to understand Reid's views on action and agency. Section 2 draws upon two of our coauthored works: "Reid on Free Will" (in Kevin Timpe, ed. *The Routledge Companion to Free Will* [Routledge, 2016: 332–42]) and "Reid's Regress" (*The Philosophical Quarterly* 69 [2019]: 678–98). Finally, I wish to thank Dale Miller, Ben Eggleston, and two anonymous referees for Cambridge University Press for their helpful feedback on a draft of the manuscript.

1 Normative Governance

Those of us who teach the history of modern philosophy are frequently asked what distinguishes one of its figures from another. Often, we offer answers such as "Hume endorses naturalistic empiricism, while Kant embraces transcendental idealism." These answers, which advert to these figures' signature positions, are not false. But we recognize that they are seriously incomplete. Philosophers embrace different positions because they ask different leading questions. Hume's leading questions in the first *Enquiry* are different from Kant's in the first *Critique*. It is this, as much as anything, that distinguishes these two figures.

Thomas Reid's *Essays on the Active Powers of Man* has its own leading questions. Reid succinctly summarizes his answers to them in the book's introduction.

> It is evidently the intention of our Maker, that man should be an active and not merely a speculative being. For this purpose, certain active powers have been given him, limited indeed in many respects, but suited to his rank and place in the creation.
>
> Our business is to manage these powers, by proposing to ourselves the best ends, planning the most proper system of conduct that is in our power, and executing it with industry and zeal. That is true wisdom; this is the very intention of our being. (EAP introduction: 5)

This passage indicates that Reid's leading questions are not those of his primary interlocutors. Unlike those of rational intuitionists such as Samuel Clarke and Richard Price, Reid's leading questions do not concern (what Ralph Cudworth calls) the "eternal and immutable" character of moral obligation. And unlike those of sentimentalists such as Francis Hutcheson and David Hume, Reid's leading questions do not concern what moves our approbation or impels us to action.[5] Rather, Reid's leading questions concern *normative governance*: How ought we as agents to govern our native capacities and active powers through the exercise of practical reason?[6] It is this question to which Reid devotes his energies in the *Active Powers*. But understanding Reid's questions requires us, his readers, to ask questions of our own. We need to know what Reid has in mind

---

[5] For present purposes, I'll understand rational intuitionism as committed to the claims that there are self-evident necessary moral truths that reason grasps via intuition, while I'll take sentimentalism to deny both that there are such truths and that reason is what grasps moral reality. Instead, sentiment is what plays the leading role in moral judgment.

[6] To be clear, I am not claiming that the rational intuitionists and the sentimentalists had nothing to say about the character of normative governance. They did. But in my view, the rationalists did not treat it as one of their leading questions. And to the extent that sentimentalists such as Hume did, their way of formulating the question does not advert to the role of practical reason. See Radcliffe (2018, 16) but also compare the comments about Hutcheson on p. 212. Harris (2013) offers a helpful historical overview of the issues.

by "active powers." And we need to understand what, according to Reid, it is to manage or govern these powers well. Addressing these questions is my project in this section.

1.1 Active Power and the Principles of Action

The passage quoted above might lead one to expect Reid to begin his discussion by explaining what he has in mind by the active powers, as these are what make us "active beings." This is not what Reid does. Instead, he begins by discussing the notion of active *power*. Moreover, it is evident from his discussion that Reid does not use the phrase "active powers" as the plural of "active power." As we'll see in section 2, according to Reid, active power is our executive practical capacity. It is that through the exertion of which agents regulate their wills (EAP I.i). There are not, in Reid's view, different kinds of active power. There is simply one kind of thing: active power. It follows that Reid is using the terms "active power" and "active powers" to refer to different kinds of things. While the former refers to our executive practical capacity, the latter must refer to what this capacity regulates. These are what Reid elsewhere calls the "principles of action."[7] Reid's considered view, then, is that active power is the executive practical capacity we exercise in order to regulate (a certain subset of) the principles of action. What, though, are the principles of action? And how would an agent govern them well?

Like many moderns, Reid uses the term "principle" in an impressively wide variety of ways. When used to theorize about action, the term can refer to an ability to act, a tendency to act, a psychological state or event that produces action, an end of action, or a practical norm or standard that directs action. When Reid says that our task is to govern the principles of action, he does not have all these meanings in mind. He means that we are to regulate a certain range of our practical abilities, tendencies, and psychological states and events by conforming to normative standards. Stated somewhat paradoxically, Reid's view is that our task is to regulate the principles of action (understood in one way) by employing, through the exercise of active power, the principles of action (understood in another way).

We do not know to what degree Reid was familiar with medieval thinkers such as Ockham and Scotus. However that may be, Reid's account of what it is to regulate the principles of action is situated within a broadly Scotist understanding of practical agency.[8] According to the Scotist approach, the ethical life

---

[7] There is one place where Reid uses the terms "powers" and "principles" interchangeably; see EAP (III.iii.viii: 193).

[8] Broadie (2000) called this to my attention.

concerns how we ought to live, and has two primary dimensions: the pursuit of what Reid calls one's "good on the whole" (or one's well-being) and conformance to "moral duty."[9] Scotus called these the dual affections. Reid calls them the *rational principles of action*.[10]

I'll explain why Reid distinguishes these two principles later. For now, it will be helpful to offer a more exact (albeit abstract) characterization of the central claim that Reid makes in his introduction: our task as human beings is to excellently manage or regulate a certain range of the principles of action by conforming to the rational principles of action. This is the core of normative governance.

1.2 The First Rational Principle of Action: Our Good on the Whole

I begin this subsection by calling attention to an easily overlooked feature of Reid's treatment of our good on the whole: the mere fact that Reid devotes so much attention to the topic at all. One finds no comparable discussion of the issue among nearly all of his primary interlocutors. Although Reid's work is driven by deep rationalist impulses, none of the rational intuitionists devotes sustained attention to the character of our good on the whole. (Even those who fall within Reid's lineage, such as Moore, Ross, and A. C. Ewing, do not discuss the topic in any detail.) And among Reid's primary interlocutors who fall outside the main lines of the rational intuitionist tradition, such as Shaftesbury, Adam Smith, and Hume, only Hume discusses the issue in any detail.[11] Predictably, Hume's view diverges sharply from Reid's. Hume endorses hedonism (roughly, the view that pleasure is the only good). Reid rejects it. In doing so, Reid breaks with nearly the entire modern tradition, spanning from Hobbes, Locke, Hutcheson, Hume, Kant, and Mill to Sidgwick, which endorses some form of hedonism.[12]

---

[9] As noted in the Introduction, I distinguish *ethics*, which concerns how we ought to live, from *morality*, which concerns a set of norms, virtues, ideals, and the like that have a certain content. This content is captured by a range of platitudes that inform us that, for example, killing for pleasure is wrong, preying upon the weak is wrong, and so forth.

[10] Reid writes that the rational principles of action "have no existence in beings not endowed with reason, and, in all their exertions, require, not only intention and will, but judgment or reason" (EAP III.iii.i: 152).

[11] See Hume's four essays on happiness in Hume (1777/1987). Butler is the other exception. Maurer (2019) canvasses what the British Moralists say about self-love, but notes that they have different things in mind by "self-love," most of which do not concern what Reid calls our good on the whole.

[12] Following Sidgwick, Irwin (2006, 501–2) interprets Butler as being committed to a form of hedonism. Irwin also attributes a version of the view to Price (717).

It is worth saying why. One finds in Reid nothing like an extended engagement with hedonism. But what he does say is interesting for two interrelated reasons. First, it brings to light some distinctive and easily overlooked elements of his methodology that help to explain why Reid rejected rival views such as hedonism. And, second, the reasons Reid offers for rejecting rival views such as hedonism provide helpful resources for understanding his own positive view.

According to the dominant characterization of Reid's approach to theorizing, we are to appeal to the principles of common sense—roughly, claims that ordinary agents must take for granted in their everyday lives. This approach to theorizing, as I'll emphasize in section 3, informs much of what Reid has to say about the second rational principle of action, the principle of duty. But it does not characterize what Reid says about our good on the whole. And it does not characterize what he says when engaging with hedonism. Reid's engagement with hedonism is more nearly Aristotelian. It instructs us not to appeal to the principles of common sense but to take up the third-person perspective on another's life.

As a practical agent, it makes sense for you to ask whether pleasure is the only (or the ultimate) good. But in raising this question, Reid writes, you ought to begin not by simply asking yourself whether you should pursue a life of pleasure. We typically don't have the requisite experience or critical perspective on our own lives to answer that question well. We sometimes do not know what is best for ourselves. And you should not, Reid further suggests, begin by merely asking yourself how a stranger would answer the question of whether you should pursue a life of pleasure. Such a person is too distant in relation to help you answer the question well. Instead, Reid maintains, begin by asking yourself what a "wise man" would recommend for the friend whom "he loves as his own soul." The wise person has both enough critical distance from and familiarity with a friend to render the appropriate advice. The advice the wise person would offer is to pursue a life not of mere pleasure but of "real virtue and worth." It follows, Reid says, that the wise person judges a life dedicated to virtue to "be best ... on the whole" (EAP III.iii.iii: 162, 163).

But how would the wise agent know that? According to Reid, such a person would know it by reflecting on the diachronic elements of practical agency, to which he or she has experiential access.

In the first part of life, Reid writes, "we have many enjoyments of various kinds ... They consist in the exercise of our senses and powers of motion, the gratification of our appetites, and the exertions of our kind affections" (EAP III.iii.ii: 155). But "when we grow to understanding," we "reflect upon what is past, and, by the lamp of experience, discern what will probably happen in time to come. We find that many things which we eagerly desired, were too dearly purchased, and that things grievous for the present, like nauseous medicines may be salutary in the issue" (EAP III.iii. ii: 155).[13] Coming to these conclusions is no simple exercise in optimizing preference satisfaction. And it is not merely a matter of employing instrumental reason in order to determine the most effective means to satisfy our preferences (EAP III.iii.i). Rather, the exercise of this aspect of agency consists in determining, by consulting and reflecting carefully upon experience, what has enduring worth, and aligning our preferences so that they are oriented toward it. Reid puts the point as follows: the "right application of this principle to our conduct requires an extensive prospect of human life, and a correct judgment and estimate of its goods and evils, with respect to their intrinsic worth and dignity, their constancy and duration, and their attainableness" (EAP III.iii.iii: 163).

What Reid says here explains why he doesn't appeal to anything like common sense when addressing questions about the character of our good on the whole. There is no sense in which the information needed to determine how to achieve one's good on the whole is *common*, accessible to the ordinary person merely by reflecting on what she takes for granted in her ordinary comings and goings. Instead, the relevant information is what would be accessible to the wise person who bears the right sort of relationship to the person who is trying to determine how to live her life. That is how we discover both that pleasure is not the only (or ultimate) good and that a life of virtue that concerns what has "dignity and worth" is what we should pursue. To the contemporary reader, this approach might seem unremarkable. But as Colin Heydt has emphasized in recent work, Reid located himself within the Protestant natural law (or deontological) tradition.[14] This tradition firmly rejected the Aristotelian methodology with its appeals to the verdicts of the practically wise agent, emphasizing instead the evidentness of ethical principles to the plain person. The fact that Reid, who belongs to the Protestant natural law (or deontological) tradition, threw in his lot with the Aristotelians regarding knowledge of our good on the whole is notable.

---

[13] Reid continues, "We learn to observe the connection of things, and the consequences of our actions; and, taking an extended view of our existence, past, present, and future, we correct our first notions of good and ill, and form the conception of what is good or ill upon the whole; which must be estimated not from the present feeling, or from the present animal desire or aversion, but from a due consideration of its consequences, certain or probable, during the whole of our existence" (EAP III.iii.ii: 155).

[14] Heydt (2018, ch. 1). The main figure in the Protestant natural law (or deontological) tradition, according to Heydt, is Pufendorf. I take the Protestant natural law (deontological) tradition and the rational intuitionist tradition to be closely aligned but distinct. A key difference is that one could be a rational intuitionist and be a consequentialist.

I'll return to this last point when discussing the principle of duty. But for now, let me call attention to Reid's repeated insistence that the practically wise agent concerns himself with what has "real virtue" and "intrinsic worth and dignity." While Reid's positive view regarding our good on the whole is sufficiently multifaceted that it resists ready categorization, these claims indicate the general thrust of his position. It is broadly perfectionist: our good on the whole consists in exercising our native capacities in order to pursue and take delight in what is of genuine "dignity and worth" (EAP introduction: 6). In a discussion of what she calls a meaningful life, Susan Wolf writes that such a life is one where "subjective attraction meets objective attractiveness."[15] I believe this slogan comes fairly close to describing what Reid has in mind by our good on the whole.

In identifying Reid's view as broadly perfectionist, we gain important insight into how he thinks of our good on the whole. But the insight is limited because we don't know much about which states and activities are (or are not) constituents of our good on the whole or the commitments agents must make in order to position themselves to achieve these goods. What we do know is that, in Reid's view, virtue lies at the core of our good on the whole. We also know why. The awareness of "integrity" (or excellent moral character), Reid writes, "would most justly claim the preference to all other enjoyments the human mind is capable of, on account of its dignity, the intenseness of the happiness it affords, its stability and duration, its being in our power, and its being proof against all accidents of time and fortune" (EAP III.iii.vii: 183).[16] Reid's assumption seems to be that, in the "well-disposed mind," what is most worth pursuing is what produces the most pleasure. A person with such a mind is aware of the great worth of achieving moral excellence, which occasions commensurate delight in the achievement, which occasions even further pleasure in the fact that he delights in what merits such delight. Joy in the well-lived life compounds.

In identifying the virtuous life so closely with our good on the whole, one might wonder whether Reid has simply appropriated the ancients' understanding of our good on the whole. The debt is unmistakable. But the appropriation is selective, as there are two primary ways in which Reid's thinking departs from commitments one finds in the ancients. Each contributes to the distinctive flavor of Reid's broadly perfectionist view.

First, while Reid's methodology is (in important respects) Aristotelian, he rejects the Aristotelian tradition's understanding of what virtue is. That

---

[15] Wolf (2015, 112).

[16] Elsewhere, Reid writes that virtue "produces a kind of self approbation," which is "the balm of life" (EAP III.iii.iii: 159; III.ii. iii: 109) and that the delight experienced in achieving this ideal is "the highest pleasure of all" (EAP III.iii.vii: 183).

understanding is one that embraces eudaimonism—roughly, the view according to which an agent's fundamental reasons for acting in some way (including dedicating oneself to a life of virtue) are that doing so would contribute to her own well-being.

Reid's rejection of eudaimonism is predicated on the claim that the virtuous agent must be wholeheartedly committed to the life of virtue. Charitably understood, this involves more than simply having resolved to perform one's obligations, as Reid sometimes claims (EAP III.ii: 66, 72). It means committing oneself to being morally excellent, where this often involves going beyond the call of duty and performing one's duties in ways that are admirable (EAP V.iv). Moral excellence of this sort, however, must be counterfactually stable. It is incompatible with selectively deviating from virtue when doing so is advantageous (say, because doing so avoids serious suffering or secures some great advantage for oneself). But if an agent were to commit herself to eudaimonism, it is difficult to see how a commitment to a virtuous life could be counterfactually stable. For, presumably, it is possible for such an agent to realize that deviating from virtue can occasionally be the best way to realize one's good on the whole. But because eudaimonism directs an agent to dedicate herself to whatever life that would contribute to her well-being, it would direct such an agent to deviate from virtue when doing so contributes to her good on the whole (EAP III.iii.iv). This would not be a wholehearted commitment to virtue in the sense specified above.

Two conclusions follow. One is that committing oneself to a virtuous life in light of eudaimonism would make it impossible to be genuinely virtuous and, so, to achieve one's good on the whole. That, in Reid's judgment, is sufficient reason to reject the view (EAP III.iii.iv). The other is that Reid's virtue-centered perfectionism has this paradoxical consequence: acting in order to realize one's good on the whole involves committing oneself to projects such that it's not the case that one's fundamental reasons for committing oneself to these projects is that they realize one's good on the whole. Butler reached a similar conclusion when arguing against egoist views. Butler's conclusion more or less falls out of Reid's virtue-centered perfectionism.

The concern that Reid expresses in the argument stated above trades upon the possibility that an agent could discover a lack of alignment between virtue and one's good on the whole. One could reject such a possibility on the grounds that one's good on the whole consists in nothing more than a life of virtue. This is the view endorsed by the Stoics, and it brings us to the second respect in which Reid's positive view departs from central commitments that one finds in the ancients.

Reid's sympathies with Stoicism run deep. But, unlike the Stoics, Reid holds that our good on the whole does not wholly consist in the life of virtue and the pleasure we experience in living such a life. Rather, it consists in the enjoyment of a wide variety of life-goods, ranging from the enjoyment of good character, warm domestic relations, and "the reciprocal exercise of kind affections" (EAP III.ii.iii: 109) to aesthetic excellence (see EIP VIII). Under a plausible reading of his treatment of justice, Reid expands this list yet further when he writes,

> [A]n innocent man has a right to the safety of his person and family, a right to his liberty and reputation, a right to his goods, and to fidelity to engagements made with him. To say that he has a right to these things, has precisely the same meaning as to say, that justice requires that he should be permitted to enjoy them, or that it is unjust to violate them. For injustice is the violation of right, and justice is, to yield to every man what is his right. (EAP V.v: 313)

The implicit assumption here seems to be twofold. First, when agents are deprived of such things as liberty, safety, reputation, and the like, then they are deprived of what matters or has worth. For if these things did not matter or have worth, then agents would not have natural rights against others that they not deprive them of these things. Of course there are many things that matter or have worth to which agents do not have natural rights, such as owning towering sequoias and Renaissance works of art. So why do agents have natural rights to the things that Reid lists? It is because—and this is the second assumption— they are elements of their good on the whole. To be deprived of such things as one's liberty, safety, or reputation is to be deprived of aspects of one's well-being.

Unlike both hedonism and Stoicism, then, Reid's view regarding our good on the whole is pluralistic, encompassing the enjoyment of a variety of life-goods. The enjoyment of some of these goods, Reid acknowledges, often lies outside our control. We become incapacitated, loved ones unexpectedly die, reputations are ruined, the beauty produced by our hands is destroyed. The Stoics saw the implications of such a pluralistic view clearly; important parts of our well-being would be outside our direct or even indirect control. Their response was to radically shrink the number of life-goods that constitute human well-being: our well-being consists solely in the life of virtue and the pleasure found therein. This option is not available to Reid. But, interestingly, Reid does not settle for the conclusion that there is a fairly tight but contingent connection between achieving moral excellence and our good on the whole. At the end of his chapter "Observations concerning conscience," Reid raises a challenge to his own view (EAP III.iii.viii). Having the challenge before us will enable us to appreciate yet another layer of Reid's position.

Suppose we understand the phrase the "prudent agent" to stand for someone who exercises practical reason well. Reid notes

Being virtuous is a primary component of achieving one's good on the whole.

Being virtuous and achieving one's good on the whole can conflict in circumstances that we may well encounter. For example, an agent may find himself in situations in which living a virtuous life renders the achievement of goods such as bodily integrity and warm domestic relations impossible.

In the prudent agent, awareness of the possibility of such conflict often occasions deep and painful anxiety, which is incompatible with achieving one's good on the whole.

These three claims, Reid charges, present the prudent agent with a practical challenge. According to Reid, there is no way to achieve one's good on the whole without being virtuous. But being virtuous appears poised to undercut the very conditions necessary for achieving one's good on the whole. That is because achieving one's good on the whole is incompatible with being subject to the type of deep and painful anxiety in which one is aware that two of one's life-projects, being virtuous and achieving one's good on the whole, may very well collide (EAP III.iii.v: 168).

The Stoic solution was to eliminate the possibility of conflict. Reid's proposed solution is theistic. The proposal does not consist in providing an argument for the existence of a Deity who guarantees the coincidence between virtue and happiness. These arguments, Reid writes, "are not of such Strength but that they may leave some doubt even in the Minds of wise and thinking Men" (EIP: 629). Instead, the proposal appeals to the character of prudence itself and claims about virtue with which we are now familiar.

To achieve one's good on the whole, one must be wholeheartedly and, so, stably committed to being virtuous. Such a commitment consists in committing oneself to the achievement of moral excellence under conditions of doubt. These conditions are ones in which rational agents can easily doubt whether conflict between achieving one's good on the whole and moral excellence will be resolved. The prudent agent, however, realizes that such stable commitment can be achieved by acting under the assumption that her ultimate well-being lies in the hands of Another. By trusting its handling of her life, such an agent can live "without any painful anxiety about future events" (EAP III.iii.v: 168). Suppose we call a reason *welfare-enabling* if it is such that, by conforming to it, one thereby positions oneself to achieve one's good on the whole. Reid's contention is that the prudent agent has a welfare-enabling reason to commit herself to there being a God who will resolve any apparent conflicts between achieving her good on the whole and being virtuous. Like Kant, then, Reid proposes that something like moral faith lies at the core of agency that effectively pursues the achievement of moral excellence and, so, one's good on the whole.[17] As Reid notes, the strategy just outlined is available to only some of his readers. For only some will find themselves able to share Reid's theological convictions.

I have been pursuing an interpretation of Reid's thinking regarding our good on the whole that highlights some of its more unusual dimensions. One such dimension is Reid's Aristotelian methodology, which is decidedly out of step with Reid's commitment to the Protestant natural law (or deontological) tradition. Another unusual dimension is the catholicity of Reid's approach, which blends perfectionism, nonhedonism, virtue-centered pluralism about life-goods, and something like theistically infused Stoicism. Let me close this subsection by drawing attention to yet another unusual dimension of Reid's position.

In several passages, Reid introduces the idea that we may come to know what our good on the whole is not by consulting the advice of the practically wise agent but by reflecting on the human constitution:

> It is therefore a most important part of the philosophy of the human mind, to have a distinct and just view of the various principles of action, which the Author of our being has planted in our nature, to arrange them properly, and to assign to every one its rank.
>
> By this it is, that we may discover the end of our being, and the part which is assigned us upon the theatre of life. (EAP III.i.i: 75)

Later, when presenting his list of the first principles of morals, Reid reiterates this idea:

> From the constitution of every species of the inferior animals, and especially from the active principles which nature has given them, we easily perceive the manner of life for which nature intended them; and they uniformly act the part to which they are led by their constitution, without any reflection upon it, or intention of obeying its dictates. Man only, of the inhabitants of this world, is made capable of observing his own constitution, what kind of life it is made for, and of acting according to that intention or contrary to it. He only is capable of yielding an intentional obedience to the dictates of his nature, or of rebelling against them. (EAP V.i: 273; *cp*. V.vi: 333)

In these passages Reid commits himself to a robust form of teleology according to which, by consulting our constitution, we can determine how we should act and live. Reid's view is not that living according to one's nature consists simply in conforming to one's motives or tendencies. The relevant motives or tendencies must be of a certain kind. They must be original to our constitution,

---

[17] Cuneo (2010) pursues the issue in greater detail.

uncorrupted, and expressed to their "natural degree" (EAP III.ii.vi).[18] In principle, they include what Reid calls the mechanical, animal, and rational motives.

What Reid says in these passages represents yet another respect in which his position differs from other rational intuitionist and broadly deontological views; to my knowledge, no prominent advocate of these views advances anything like what Reid says here.[19] But what Reid says also introduces tension into his position, which we can make manifest by considering two claims that Reid endorses:

> **Worth-Dignity**: One's good on the whole consists in responding appropriately to what has worth and dignity.

and:

> **Teleology**: One's good on the whole consists in living in accordance with one's nature, including conforming to one's original motives. This is something we can ascertain by reflecting carefully on our constitution.

Along the way, we've caught a glimpse of what, in Reid's view, has worth and dignity. It includes such things as a life of virtue, warm domestic relations, aesthetic excellence, relations of trust with others, and so on.

Worth-Dignity and Teleology do not fit well together. We can make their lack of fit explicit by identifying some additional assumptions about human nature with which Reid would have been sympathetic (*cp*. EAP III.ii.v). These assumptions include: Human nature includes a constellation of different tendencies. Some orient us to pursue life-goods, which have worth and dignity. Others orient us toward life-evils, such as acting violently and dominating the vulnerable, which lack such worth and dignity. Moreover, by all appearances, the latter tendencies are no less "original" than the former. But Teleology tells us that one's good on the whole consists in living in accordance with one's nature. Given the assumption that one's good on the whole is composed of what has worth and dignity, this implies either of two conclusions. The first is the Nietzschean view that activities such as dominating the vulnerable are not life-evils but life-goods that have worth and dignity. The second is that Teleology is false; one's good on the whole does not consist in living in accordance with one's nature.

Reid would have rejected both conclusions. Given Reid's commitments, the best response to the "Malevolent Motives Worry" (as we might call it) probably involves embracing a more nuanced version of Teleology. According to such

---

[18] Kroeker (2014) discusses these dimensions of Reid's thinking in greater detail.

[19] To my knowledge, only Butler, and Reid's teacher George Turnbull (1741/2008), advance claims in this vicinity.

a version, one's good on the whole consists in living in accordance with one's nature but only insofar as it sufficiently orients one toward what has worth and dignity. This response affirms the centrality of Worth-Dignity; any additional theses regarding our good on the whole, such as Teleology, must fit well with it. But a response such as this may be less than wholly satisfactory. For one could legitimately question whether a more nuanced version of Teleology does any theoretical work. At first glance, it seems like a more nuanced version of Teleology would not genuinely deepen or expand our understanding of our good on the whole, because nothing important would be lost if Reid were to reject the claim altogether.

I suspect that Reid would disagree. To see why, return to the apothegm from Susan Wolf quoted earlier, a version of which states that our good on the whole is where objective value meets subjective attraction. We can think of Reid's invocation of teleology as speaking to that part of Wolf's slogan that concerns subjective attraction. Reid's thinking seems to be that human agents don't merely happen to be attracted to what is of genuine worth. Rather, they are constituted to be so attracted and to delight in the satisfaction of this attraction. This is something we can discern from reflecting on our constitution with its various tendencies—even if we can discern that we are also attracted to what lacks such worth. In this way, there is a fit between the kind of beings we are with our repertoire of rational and affective characteristics, on the one hand, and what is of genuine worth, on the other.

This response helps to substantiate the conviction that a satisfactory account of our good on the whole must not imply that we can be easily alienated from our good on the whole. After all, if there is a close fit between what we tend toward by our constitution and elements of our good on the whole, being alienated from our good on the whole would involve failing to tend toward that to which our very nature leads us. The Malevolent Motives Worry helps us to see that the fit is not perfect. The fact that the fit is not perfect is incentive to find independent resources for identifying what has worth and dignity, such as the experience of the practically wise agent. Nonetheless, when charitably understood, Reid's invocation of teleology is designed to draw attention to the fact that our good on the whole involves a fit between what is of worth and dignity and that to which our constitution orients us.

Earlier I said that Reid's understanding of our good on the whole defies ready categorization. Reid's commitment to robustly teleological claims complicates the picture even further, revealing yet another layer of complexity in Reid's view. Without making any claims about how exactly the various elements of Reid's view hang together, we have a clearer picture of how Reid is thinking of our good on the whole. Reid's position is a virtue-centered, pluralistic version of perfectionism. We can ascertain which life-goods compose our good on the whole by consulting the advice of the practically wise agent and by reflecting on our constitution. In addition, we know that, in Reid's view, having certain types of attitudes are integral for achieving our good on the whole. Among these are a commitment to the existence of a benevolent deity. I am not aware of a name for a view regarding our good on the whole that has these same features. Given that Reid seems to be the primary architect of such a view, we probably can't go wrong in calling it the *Reidian view of the human good.*

1.3 The Second Rational Principle of Action: Duty

Our topic in the previous subsection was Reid's understanding of the first rational principle of action, our good on the whole. I now turn to the principle of duty, which is Reid's second rational principle of action.

Earlier I pointed out that Reid uses the phrase "principle of action" capaciously. Reid's capacious and, indeed, fluid use of the phrase is especially apparent in his discussion of the principle of duty. In some places, he uses the phrase "principle of duty" to refer to a norm or standard to which we are to conform. In other places, Reid speaks of the principle of duty as an end or a goal for which we act. Elsewhere, Reid uses it to advert to an original faculty or ability.

Each use of the phrase is potentially misleading. When used to designate a standard or norm, Reid's phraseology strongly suggests that there is a single thing that is *the* principle of duty. But there is no such single standard, according to Reid. Rather, there is a plurality of such standards, which Reid calls the "first principles of morals." For Reid, the phrase "the principle of duty" functions as a linguistic placeholder that adverts to these principles. When used to refer to an end, the phrase "principle of duty" suggests that the end for which we act is that of conforming to moral obligation. Reid, however, typically has more in mind than this; to act for the sake of the principle of duty often involves acting in order to be virtuous or morally excellent, which is not simply a matter of conforming to duty. Finally, when used to advert to an ability or faculty, the phrase "principle of duty" suggests that it is an ability to grasp and conform to moral duty. But the *Active Powers* makes it clear that, so understood, the principle of duty is much more than that. It is an ability that also enables agents to grasp and be motivated by moral "duty" understood as an end, which includes the morally good and the morally excellent.

Given Reid's use of terminology, I propose to structure the discussion in this subsection as follows. I'll begin by exploring the principle of duty understood as a standard and an end. (Section 3 will have more yet to say about moral standards.) I'll then turn to what Reid says about the principle understood as a faculty or ability. Toward the end of the discussion, we'll see that Reid thinks that there are important connections between the principle of duty understood in these two different ways. Reid appears to claim that the principle of duty, understood as a faculty, not only grasps but also *generates* moral reasons to act.

When Reid uses the phrase "the principle of duty" to designate moral standards, he specifies standards of two sorts. Some are (or involve) first-order moral obligations that Reid identifies, such as:

> It is prima facie wrong to wound, maim, or kill others.
> It is prima facie wrong to destroy the reputation of others.
> It is prima facie wrong to break our promises to others.[20]

and:

> In every case, we ought to act that part toward another, which we would judge to be right in him to act toward us, if we were in his circumstances and he in ours. (EAP V.i and V.v)

Others are second-order obligations concerning how we should conform to our first-order moral obligations. They include:

> We ought to use the best means we can to be well informed of our duty, by serious attention to moral instruction; by observing what we approve, and what we disapprove, in others and ourselves; by reflecting often on our own past conduct; and by deliberating cooly and impartially upon our future conduct. (EAP V.i: 271)

A striking feature of Reid's discussion of the first principles of morals is that it does not aspire to comprehensiveness or systematicity in the sense of explaining how these principles bear upon each other (EAP V.ii: 281–2).[21] (In this respect, Reid's position anticipates the type of deontological position developed by W. D. Ross.) In failing to identify the most fundamental ethical principles that explain and unify the others, Sidgwick alleged that Reid fails to even attempt what a satisfactory normative theory must accomplish.[22] Sidgwick's allegation notwithstanding, Reid's interests seem to lie elsewhere. He is more interested in establishing a pair of claims: first, the principle of duty is distinct from our good on the whole and, second, we should treat the principle of duty as authoritative. Let us consider each claim in turn.

---

[20] Hurka (2014, 70) maintains that H. A. Prichard introduces the notion of the prima facie and Ross is the first to develop it. That seems to me not quite accurate; Reid recognizes the distinction at EAP V.i, although he does not develop it.

[21] But *cp.* EAP V.i: 274–5 and III.iii.viii: 189.   [22] Sidgwick (1907, 103–4).

Reid's broadly Scotist understanding of agency commits itself to there being two distinct rational principles of action: our good on the whole and duty. Still, in a variety of passages, Reid emphasizes that the two rational principles of action are closely connected. Our good on the whole and the principle of duty "lead to the same course of conduct, and co-operate with each other" like "two fountains whose streams unite and run in the same channel" (EAP III.iii.i: 154; III.iii.v: 173). While passages such as these can make it sound as if Reid thinks of these principles as tendencies or abilities, when Reid argues that these principles are distinct, he is not thinking of them in this way. He is thinking of them as ends (EAP III.iii.i: 154; *cp.* V.vii: 360). His claim is that the end of achieving one's good on the whole is distinct from the end of achieving moral excellence.

The argument for this claim runs as follows. Begin with the observation that realizing one's good on the whole is a genuine achievement; it merits esteem. Observe, next, that the esteem it merits is of a distinctive sort: "[T]hough a steady pursuit of our own real good may, in an enlightened mind, produce a kind of virtue which is entitled to some degree of approbation, yet it can never produce the noblest kind of virtue, which claims our highest love and esteem" (EAP III.iii.iv: 165; *cp.* V.i: 272). Note, next, that achieving moral virtue involves having traits that merit our highest love and esteem (EAP III.iii.iv: 166).[23] Add, finally, the premise that, necessarily, if x and y are approbation-worthy but x merits responses of such a kind that y could not, then x and y are distinct. It follows that achieving our good on the whole and achieving virtue are different. They necessarily merit different responses.

Reid is at pains to emphasize why the achievement of these different goals merits different responses. It is because they involve agents being oriented toward what has worth and dignity in different ways and, thus, being motivated differently. A vivid way to appreciate the point is to consider actions that any agent has strong moral reason to perform. Reid proposes that "relieving an innocent out of great distress" is such an action; it is what Reid calls good "considered abstractly" (EAP V.iv: 297). An action such as this can, however, be performed in different ways. When performed in such a way that the agent concerns himself with another's worth or well-being—perhaps at "considerable expence or danger to himself"—the agent receives moral credit for its perform-ance (EAP V.iv: 298). When performed in such a way that the agent concerns

---

[23] "Our cordial love and esteem is due only to the man whose soul is not contracted within itself, but embraces a more extensive object: who loves virtue, not for her dowry only, but for her own sake; whose benevolence is not selfish, but generous and disinterested; who, forgetful of himself, has the common good at heart, not as the means only, but as the end; who abhors what is base, though he were to be a gainer by it, and loves that which is right, although he should suffer from it" (EAP III.iii.iv: 166).

himself not with these things but only (or ultimately) with his own well-being or reputation, then the agent receives no moral credit for its performance (cf. EAP III.iii.iv). In both cases, the agent will have performed an action that is good considered abstractly. And he may have achieved his good on the whole. But in only one case does he achieve moral excellence. In only one case does he merit the "highest love and esteem."

These points might seem close to moral common sense. But Reid indicates that his is not the dominant view among his interlocutors:

> [T]he formal nature and essence of that virtue which is the object of moral approbation consists neither in a prudent prosecution of our private interest, nor in benevolent affections toward others, nor in qualities useful or agreeable to ourselves or to others, nor in sympathizing with the passions and affections of others, and in attuning our own conduct to the tone of other men's passions; but it consists in living in all good conscience, that is, in using the best means in our power to know our duty, and acting accordingly. (EAP V.iv: 300–1)

This passage voices Reid's disagreement with Hobbes, Hutcheson, Hume, and Smith. His thinking seems to be that each of these figures offers an account of what renders an agent and her acts approbation-worthy. Hobbes appeals to an agent's private interest. Hutcheson appeals to benevolence. Hume and Smith appeal to what sorts of attitudes an agent's traits would evoke in a sympathetic observer. In each case, these philosophers identify some feature (or set of features) that makes an agent and her actions approbation-worthy. In Reid's view, all these figures offer at best incomplete and at worst incorrect accounts of what renders agents and their actions worthy of moral approbation. Their views are incomplete to the extent that they fail to capture what virtue is at its core and incorrect insofar as they maintain that traits are virtuous because suitably situated agents would approve of them.

If correct, Reid's verdict warrants two claims. First, achieving one's good on the whole is not identical with achieving moral excellence. While it is possible that, necessarily, pursuing one's good on the whole and moral excellence require one to perform exactly the same types of actions, the reasons for which you perform these actions needn't be identical. One can achieve moral excellence only if the ultimate reasons for which you act do not solely concern one's good on the whole. This is not true of achieving central components of one's good on the whole. It is possible to achieve a life-good such as psychic harmony even when one's ultimate reason for pursuing it is to achieve this very good.

Second, achieving moral excellence is not reducible to or fully grounded in achieving one's good on the whole. This second conclusion follows from Reid's claim that a primary component of an agent's good on the whole is the enjoyment of moral goods, such as one's own virtue. A view that attempts to fully ground moral reality in one's good on the whole would in effect attempt to ground moral obligation in itself. For the primary component of our good on the whole consists in pursuing virtue, which itself consists (at least in part) in resolving to conform to the first principles of morals, which are moral obligations. Although Reid never makes the point explicitly, this claim might partly explain why he made no attempt to meet Sidgwick's challenge of identifying some fundamental moral principle that explains and unifies the rest. It is not that Reid was a proto "anti-theorist" who saw little need for law-like systematicity when theorizing. Instead, it is probably because Reid viewed the main alternatives to his own pluralistic deontological approach as being eudaimonistic or utilitarian: we can attempt to fully ground moral principles in how acts conduce to one's own good or the aggregate good of everyone (cf. EAP V.v). But, given Reid's view of our good on the whole, whose primary components include the cultivation and enjoyment of one's own virtue, there is no satisfactory defense of such a grounding claim.

Like most philosophers, Reid does not shrink from marking distinctions that others have missed. But, as I've emphasized, Reid's aim in distinguishing the two rational principles of action is not primarily to ensure that his theory "cuts at the joints" by, say, identifying what is most fundamental in ethical reality. It is rather to identify the different practical and theoretical roles that the rational principles of action play, marking what is special about the principle of duty. We have seen one respect in which Reid believes the principle is special; achieving the end of moral excellence is worthy of our highest esteem and admiration. There is, however, another, related respect in which Reid believes the principle of duty is unique: it is normatively authoritative. And by this Reid means that *both* that the principle of duty understood as a standard and as a faculty are authoritative.

Begin with what Reid says about the authority of the principle of duty understood as a standard. A helpful way to appreciate what Reid says is by having before us the notion of a "plain person." Such an agent is one whose mental faculties are intact, and who has received a reasonably good moral education sufficiently free from corrupting influences (EAP III.iii.vii).[24] In his

---

[24] I borrow the term from MacIntyre (1988, 324). Reid writes that the plain person grasps the first principles by exercising her indigenous moral capacities together with "instruction, education, exercise, and habit" (EAP III.iii.viii: 188). MacIntyre (1988, 324–5) characterizes Reid's view thus: Reid "appealed to that in those plain persons which is independent of the particularities of their history, their institutions, or the ordering of their passions, for he appealed to that in them which he claimed to be constant and unvarying in all human nature and prior to all theorizing . . . . All plain persons of sound mind assent to one and the same set of fundamental truths as

presentation of the first principles of morals, Reid appeals to the plain person. The plain person easily grasps the first principles of morals, as they are highly evident. In his discussion of the normative authority of morality, however, Reid tends not to appeal to the plain person. That is, he tends not to claim that the authority of moral standards is self-evident to the plain person.[25] Rather, Reid appeals to the virtuous agent, the "person of honor" (EAP III.iii: 170). When asked whether moral considerations take precedence over her good on the whole, the person of honor affirms that they do:

> [T]he principle of honor is evidently superior in dignity to that of interest . . . . I take it for granted, therefore, that every man of real honor feels an abhorrence of certain actions, because they are in themselves base, and feels an obligation to certain other actions, because they are in themselves what honor requires, and this, independently of any consideration of interest or reputation. (EAP III.iii: 170)

While this passage might be misleading in one respect—to fail to conform to virtue, after all, needn't be "base"—I take Reid's central point to be that the authority of morality may be something that is not highly evident to the plain person. But morality's authority is highly evident to the person who lives her life in conformance with these principles. Because it is, the plain person should defer to the judgment of the virtuous agent, just as the novice musician defers to the judgment of the expert musician. If all goes well, with time and experience, the plain person will also be able to appreciate what the wise agent does.

What Reid says doesn't explain why the first principles of morals are authoritative; it tells us how we *know* that they are. Interestingly for our purposes, Reid's treatment of the authority of moral obligation represents yet another case in which he employs a methodology distinct from that of common sense. After all, the insights of the virtuous agent are not accessible to the plain person merely by reflecting on what she takes for granted in her day-to-day life. For the plain person, these insights are accessible only through testimony and reflection. I've emphasized that this broadly Aristotelian methodology is decidedly out of step with the dominant trends in the Protestant natural law (or deontological) tradition, which rejected the idea that moral expertise is crucial for obtaining moral knowledge. But, as already noted in our earlier discussion of eudaimonism, Reid's appropriation of the Aristotelian tradition is selective. Reid seems to have recognized that there was space to mark distinctions—such as

---

underived first principles, the truths of common sense, as soon as these truths are elicited from the mind by experience." *Cp.* MacIntyre (1990, 175). It seems to me that what Reid says in EAP III.iii.vii clearly belies this interpretation. *Cp.* Davis (2006, 69–73, 110–31).

[25] The one exception of which I'm aware is found at EAP III.iii.viii: 192. Interestingly, in this passage, Reid speaks of the authority of not moral standards but conscience.

between the Aristotelian tradition's methodology and its positive claims about why we should be virtuous—where his interlocutors in the Protestant natural law tradition did not.

At the outset of this subsection, I said that I would focus on the principle of duty understood in two ways: as an end or a standard, on the one hand, and as a faculty or an ability, on the other. To this point, I have had my eye on the principle of duty understood as a standard and an end, asking why Reid thinks that our good on the whole and the principle of duty so understood are distinct, and why he thinks that the latter should be treated as authoritative. I want now to turn to the principle of duty understood as a faculty or an ability. As it turns out, the Aristotelian idea that we should defer to authoritative verdicts directly connects to Reid's discussion of the principle of duty understood as a faculty or an ability.

Reid's central claim here is that the ability to grasp and conform to moral standards is authoritative. Sometimes, following the sentimentalists, Reid calls this faculty the moral sense. Elsewhere, following Butler, Reid calls it "conscience," writing that

> [i]ts intention is manifestly implied in its office; which is, to show us what is good, what is bad, and what indifferent in human conduct. . . . Conscience prescribes measures to every appetite, affection, and passion, and says to every other principle of action, So far thou mayest go, but no further . . . .
>
> Other principles of action may have more strength, but this only has authority. Its sentence makes us guilty to ourselves . . . . It is evident therefore, that this principle has, from its nature, an authority to direct and determine with regard to our conduct; to judge; to acquit, or to condemn, and even to punish; an authority which belongs to no other principle of the human mind. (EAP III.iii.viii: 192)

This passage is at once fascinating and perplexing. It admits of at least two interpretations—one deflationary, the other inflationary. Let me close by considering these two interpretations.

According to a deflationary reading, we must read past Reid's rhetoric. Conscience is authoritative only insofar as it is a trustworthy faculty for grasping authoritative moral standards. Any authority conscience might have is wholly parasitic on the authority of the moral standards it grasps.[26] Reid says things that support this deflationary reading. For example, immediately after the

---

[26] Irwin (2006, 493) appears to read Butler similarly. Schneewind (1998, 347, 352–3) offers a very different reading of Butler's view regarding the authority of conscience, characterizing conscience as the voice of God in the agent. If correct, this reading would probably require an interpretation of Reid's views about the authority of conscience that differs from that suggested above.

passage just quoted, Reid writes that the "authority of conscience over the other active principles of the mind ... implies no more than this, that in all cases a man ought to do his duty" (EAP III.iii.viii: 192). Add now that the idea of an authoritative *ability* or faculty is hardly transparent. It is relatively easy to characterize what it is for an agent to be authoritative: it is for that agent to have a certain kind of normative standing—what the medievals called a *potestas*. Such a normative standing, in turn, consists in having rights of a certain range. Abilities or faculties, however, are not agents; they have no rights. Because they do not, it is unclear what the authority of an ability or faculty would be. The deflationary reading endeavors to avoid these puzzling features of Reid's discussion.

The inflationary reading, in contrast, takes Reid's rhetoric at more or less face value. According to this interpretation, Reid is claiming that, in every case in which a plain person judges that she morally ought to act in a given way, conscience issues the demand that she act in that way. In every case in which such a person judges that she morally ought not to act in a given way, conscience issues the demand that she not act in that way. When such an agent knowingly transgresses her duty, conscience condemns her as guilty. And so on. In short, conscience is a faculty that issues demands that, when all goes well, generate reasons that correspond to the moral reasons that an agent already has. It also issues verdicts (such as *guilty* or *innocent*) that, when all goes well, correspond to the moral status that an agent already has.

For some of the considerations just offered, I find the inflationary reading puzzling. But there may be a way to make sense of some of what Reid is saying. Suppose we agree that the authority of conscience cannot reside in its having rights of a certain range, because conscience cannot have rights. And suppose we agree that conscience's authority does not reside in the fact that the reasons it generates "preempt" other reasons. That is, suppose we agree that the reasons generated by conscience are not like those generated by an authoritative law to behave in some way, which exclude other considerations in favor of behaving in that way.[27] This last supposition seems warranted if only because conscience takes the first principles of morals reasons as inputs and supplements them by issuing directives and verdicts that correspond to them. It does not preempt them. The reasons generated by conscience, then, appear to be of a distinctive sort.

We can identify their distinctiveness by reflecting on a familiar case. Imagine that you and I are plain persons. You judge that you morally should act in way x, and I judge that I morally ought to act in way y (these ways needn't be different).

---

[27] This is the influential approach to authority developed by Raz (1986).

Now suppose your conscience demands that you act in way *x*, and my conscience demands that I act in way *y*. And suppose that these demands generate reasons that correspond to the moral judgments you make and the moral judgments that I make. The practical reasons generated by these demands appear to be irreducibly first-personal. This is because what your conscience dictates is a reason only for you, while what my conscience dictates is a reason only for me. By their very nature, these first-personal reasons cannot be shared.[28]

But if that is so, then we might get a sense of why, according to Reid, conscience enjoys a type of authority. The thinking is that conscience is an original faculty and, so, trustworthy. Given that the proper conditions hold, conscience tends to render the correct moral demands and verdicts:

> Every man in his senses believes his eyes, his ears, and his other senses. He believes his consciousness, with respect to his own thoughts and purposes, his memory, with regard to what is past, his understanding, with regard to abstract relations of things, and his taste, with regard to what is elegant and beautiful. And he has the same reason, and, indeed, is under the same necessity of believing the clear and unbiased dictates of his conscience, with regard to what is honorable and what is base. (EAP III.iii.vi: 180)

The "dictates" of conscience generate irreducibly first-personal moral reasons. In this sense, conscience determines or *controls* what reasons you have to act.[29] But when a source determines or controls which trustworthy first-personal reasons you have, then it is a good candidate for being authoritative.

Think of the law or a person who holds a given office as a comparison: when the law or the person who holds that office determines or controls what trustworthy reasons you have, then the law or that figure is authoritative.[30] In the case of conscience, it generates reasons that not only supplement other reasons you might have but also are decisive in virtue of their strength and first-personal character. They are reasons for you and you alone. In saying this, I do not mean to suggest that Reid spells out this reasoning anywhere. But it appears to be a plausible way to interpret how he was thinking. The authority of conscience resides in the fact that it controls the moral reasons that an agent has.

---

[28] Zagzebski (2012, ch. 3) offers a treatment of first-personal reasons.

[29] *Cp*. Reid's comments about the will at EAP II.i. I have in mind here and in what follows reasons that are not easily defeasible.

[30] Murphy (2001, ch. 1) articulates a view of authority along these lines. I am omitting a variety of important qualifications that Murphy includes in his discussion, perhaps the most important of which is that the control be not merely causal but constitutive.

1.4 Conclusion

Reid's leading question in the *Active Powers* asks how agents should manage the variety of psychological states and tendencies that move us to action. According to the answer he offers, we should manage them by conforming to the two rational principles of action: our good on the whole and duty. According to the interpretation on offer, Reid's claim is not simply that agents should conform to these principles. Rather, his agency-centered approach implies that having the capacity to conform to these two principles is what forms the core of rational (human) agency. Such agency is effective to the extent that it conforms to these principles to a high degree.

As for the two principles themselves, our primary objective has been to understand them. Reid's view regarding our good on the whole is broadly perfectionist but resists categorization, given its diverse commitments. (For this reason, I've suggested we call it the Reidian account of the human good.) When it comes to the principle of duty, we've seen that Reid works with two different understandings of what it is. According to the first, the principle is actually a constellation of moral standards (which can also function as ends). According to the second, it is an original faculty of the mind, which Reid calls the "moral sense" or "conscience." If the interpretation of Reid's views just offered is correct, Reid believes that the principle of duty is in both respects authoritative. We know that moral standards are authoritative via the testimony of the virtuous agent. The authority of the moral sense lies in its capacity to control the moral reasons an agent has by issuing first-personal reasons that coincide with the first principles of morals.

2 Action, Motives, Power

According to an agency-centered approach to ethical theorizing, ethical questions are to be pursued in light of and informed by substantive commitments regarding the character of agency and action. Reid's approach to ethical theorizing is agency-centered. In the previous section, I explored the role of the rational principles of action in Reid's agency-centered approach. In this section, I explore dimensions of Reid's position at the intersection of agency and action.

There are at least two reasons why Reid develops an agency-centered approach. The first is Reid's conviction that a satisfactory ethical theory should incorporate the insights from the broadly sentimentalist tradition. Rather than ignore issues in moral psychology, as nearly all the rational intuitionist theories did, Reid endeavors to take what is valuable from the sentimentalists (and Butler), modifying it to suit his purposes. The second reason is that Reid accepts a pair of claims that links action to ethical evaluation.[31] According to the first of these claims, agents are beholden to moral obligations only if they can rightly be held accountable for conforming or failing to conform to them. According to the second, agents can rightly be held accountable for performing an action only if they were free with respect to performing it (or were free with respect to performing some other action that is suitably related to the performance of the action in question). These two commitments require Reid to address a range of difficult issues in the philosophy of action.

Reid is a sufficiently lucid writer that his readers do not face the types of exegetical challenges they must when interpreting figures such as Hume and Kant. Nonetheless, there are obscurities in and puzzling features of Reid's discussion of action. I propose to explore three. The first concerns what Reid means by "action." Reid works with competing characterizations of action that not only can make understanding his views challenging but also expose his views to powerful objections. The second puzzling feature of Reid's discussion is what Reid has in mind when he calls something a "motive." In this case, Reid embraces competing characterizations of what motives are, which are challenging to reconcile. The third is what Reid commits himself to when he says that agents are causes endowed with active power. While the notion of active power lies at the heart of Reid's theorizing, understanding it requires considerable interpretive effort.

My topic, then, is Reid on action, motives, and active power. What will emerge from our discussion is that Reid crafts what he says on these subjects in light of his conviction that human beings have robust freedom. The interpretive puzzles that arise mostly concern fitting what Reid says on these

---

[31] Both are present in Reid's "second argument for moral liberty" (EAP IV.vii).

subjects with this conviction. But there is no shortcut to solving these inter-pretive puzzles. Arriving at a satisfactory interpretation of what Reid says will require us to enter into the thickets of textual interpretation, at points drawing distinctions that Reid himself did not mark. I am hopeful that these efforts will pay dividends, enabling us not only to understand what Reid says but also to arrive at an interpretation according to which Reid's views hang together cohesively.

2.1 Action

Let me begin by regimenting some terminology.

Call any mental or bodily change in the world produced by an agent (or some part of an agent) the actualization of a *behavior-state*. Your digesting this morning's breakfast is the actualization of a behavior-state, as it is (in some sense) due to you (or some part of you). Similarly, your poring over a map of the Napa Valley is also the actualization of a behavior-state. But there is a crucial difference between the two cases: while digesting breakfast is not an action, closely examining a map of the Napa Valley is. What explains the difference between these two cases? Why do the actualizations of some behavior-states count as an agent's actions while the actualizations of others do not?

Reid has a very simple answer to these questions: the actualization of a behavior-state counts as your action just in case and because you are its efficient cause (EAP I.i: 13). This is Reid's answer to the two questions raised above, which form the core of what we might call the *action problem*. Let's now add that Reid works with a restricted account of what can count as an action. The actualization of a behavior-state counts as an action, according to Reid, if and only if it is free (EAP IV.i: 267, IV.iii: 212).

Reid's answer to the action problem presupposes a distinction between what he calls "efficient" and "physical" causality (*cf.* EAP I.vii: 41 and Cor 178). Reid adopts the notion of an efficient cause from thinkers such as Samuel Clarke.[32] An efficient cause is what some today would call an *agent cause*. An agent cause, in turn, is something endowed with active power—what I, in the section 1, referred to as your executive practical capacity. Because you are an agent, Reid holds that you are an agent cause and, hence, endowed with active power. Reid adopts the notion of a physical cause from Hume. Roughly, a physical cause is an event of some type that is connected by a law of nature to an event of some other type. When you throw a baseball at a window, for

---

[32] The core notion, however, stretches back to the ancients. See Frede (1987). Reid's terminology is confusing to contemporary readers because what he calls efficient causation (namely, agent causation) is not what we today call efficient causation. What we mean by "efficient causation" is what Reid calls physical causation.

example, your throwing the baseball is a physical cause of the window's shattering, because events of the first type (i.e., throwing a baseball at a window) are connected by a law of nature to events of another type (i.e., a window's shattering upon impact).

Agent (or efficient) causality and physical causality appear to be very different. Agent causes are not events; they are substances. And physical causes are not agents; they are events. Surprisingly, though, Reid maintains that the two types of causes are very closely linked, holding that the only genuine causality in the world consists in the exercise of agent causality. If Reid is right, your deciding to throw a baseball at a window comes about through an exertion of your active power. You are this event's agent cause. That the ball flies through the air and shatters the window upon impact is, Reid says, due to the exertion of God's active power. For the "physical laws of nature are the rules according to which the Deity commonly acts in his natural government of the world; and, whatever is done according to them, is not done by man, but by God, either immediately, or by instruments under his direction" (EAP IV.xi: 251).

Reid, then, endorses a version of semi-occasionalism according to which both you and God are the agent causes of the ball's shattering the window. (I say the view is a version of *semi*-occasionalism because Reid allows that both human beings and God are agent causes. In contrast, traditional occasionalist views maintain that God is the only agent cause.[33]) While the notion of an agent cause is central to Reid's thinking, Reid makes no effort to define the notion. Instead, Reid specifies an array of conditions that something must satisfy in order to be an agent cause. Among these is that an agent cause have active power, and that active power must come with options: "Power to produce an effect," Reid writes, "implies power not to produce it" (EAP I.v: 29). Following Gideon Yaffe, let us call this condition:

> **Power to Do Otherwise**: If an agent has the power to act in a certain way, then he also has the power not to act in that way.[34]

Power to Do Otherwise affords an even clearer understanding of Reid's answer to the action problem: it tells us that the actualization of any behavior-state of which someone is an agent cause must be such that that person had the power to not actualize that behavior-state when he did. Although this is helpful, we still don't know exactly what sorts of behavior-states, according to Reid, satisfy this condition. Do mental events, such as imagining the vineyards of the Napa

---

[33] Van Cleve (2015, ch. 14) provides helpful discussion regarding Reid's semi-occasionalism. As Van Woudenberg (2004, 218–19) indicates, the view that all causality is agential is motivated by Reid's Newtonian conviction that matter, which is nonagential, is inert. See EAP I.vi.

[34] See Yaffe (2004, ch. 2)

Valley, as well as bodily movements, such as throwing baseballs, satisfy Power to Do Otherwise and, hence, count as actions?

Reid says different things on this matter. In some places, he acknowledges that there is an ordinary understanding of action that is broad according to which the actualization of a wide array of behavior-states, such as deciding to visit the Napa Valley and actually visiting it, count as actions (see EAP III.i.i: 97, IV.i: 198). Call this the *wide understanding of action*. In other places, Reid acknowledges that there is a "philosophical" understanding of action according to which only the actualization of those behavior-states that consist in or are the direct consequence of an exertion of active power are actions (see EAP I.i: 13, IV.ii: 203). Because Reid holds that the direct consequence of the exertion of active power is the formation and enactment of decisions or volitions, this view implies that while your decision to visit the Napa Valley is an action, your driving there is not. Call this the *narrow understanding of action*. Sometimes Reid seems to work with the wide understanding; other times he appears to work with the narrow understanding. Each understanding has its theoretical pros and cons.

The primary virtue of the wide understanding is that it approximates our ordinary understanding of action according to which the actualization of behavior-states such as throwing baseballs, flagging down cabs, and scratching one's ear are actions and, hence, behavior-states for which we can be held accountable. The wide understanding, however, also has a downside, which is that it exposes Reid's view to counterexamples that are potentially quite damaging, given his assumption that all actions are free.

Reid would have been familiar with some of these counterexamples. The best known of these is Locke's man-in-a-locked-room scenario, which is a precursor to so-called Frankfurt-style counterexamples.[35] In Locke's presentation of the scenario, we are to imagine a man locked in a room. Although the man decides to stay in the room, he lacks the power to leave because, unbeknownst to him, the door is locked. This case provides the materials for the following objection to Reid's view:

1. The actualization of a behavior-state B counts as an agent's action time t only if B satisfies Power to Do Otherwise at t. (from Reid's answer to the action problem and Power to Do Otherwise)

2. The man-in-the-locked-room's behavior of staying in the locked room doesn't satisfy Power to Do Otherwise: he has the power to stay in the room but lacks the power to refrain from staying in the room. (assumption)

---

[35] Locke (1690/1975, II.xxi.10: 238) and Frankfurt (1969).

3. So when the man-in-the-locked-room decides to stay in the room, his behavior of staying in the room does not count as his action. (from 1, 2)

No one, however, forces the man-in-the-locked-room to stay in the room; he stays by his own volition. So it is very plausible to hold that

4. The man-in-the-locked-room's behavior of staying in the room does count as his action. (assumption)

This claim, however, implies that

5. (1) is false: it's not the case that the actualization of a behavior-state B counts as an agent's action at t only if B satisfies Power to Do Otherwise at t. (from 1–4)

Given Reid's assumption that the actualization of a behavior-state counts as an action if and only if it is free, 5 implies:

The man-in-the-locked-room's behavior of staying in the locked room is not a free action.

This appears to be a problem for the wide understanding of action. For according to this understanding of action, it looks as if in Locke's scenario the man's staying in the room is a free action.

What I earlier referred to as the narrow understanding of action sidesteps this objection completely, as it holds that the exertion of active power and the formation and enaction of volitions are the only types of action that agents perform. If this is right, the correct description of the man-in-the-locked-room scenario focuses on the man's formation of volitions through the exertion of his active power. When the man decides to stay, his decision results from the exertion of his active power. But when he decides this, he could decide otherwise; he could decide not to stay. Of course, he would be unable to execute his decision and leave because he would discover that the door to the room in which he's staying is locked. Still, his volition to stay satisfies Power to Do Otherwise. Given Reid's further claim that the only types of actions are free actions, his decision to stay is a free action.

There is a price for accepting the narrow view of action. This view not only radically constricts the range of behavior-states that can count as actions, but also "internalizes" action, implying that none of the behaviors that we commonly call actions, such as throwing baseballs, flagging down cabs, and scratching one's ear, could be actions strictly so called (*cf.* EAP I.i and I.vii: 36 with IV.i). For a philosopher who prided himself in defending common sense, this would be an unwelcome result.

The puzzle facing us, then, is that Reid works with two different notions of action, neither of which appears to be fully satisfactory given his aims. Reid says some things that suggest a way of blunting the force of this concern. When presenting the narrow understanding of action, Reid acknowledges that, strictly speaking, the actualization of many behavior-states, such as throwing objects, do not count as actions. Nonetheless, Reid continues, agents can be held morally responsible for the actualization of such behavior-states:

> That there is an established harmony between our willing certain motions of our bodies, and the operations of the nerves and muscles which produces those motions, is a fact known by experience. This volition is an act of the mind. But whether this act of the mind have any physical effect upon the nerves and muscles, or whether it be only an occasion of their being acted upon by some other efficient [cause], according to the established laws of nature, is hid from us.

Still,

> the man who knows that such an event depends upon his will, and who deliberately wills to produce it is, in the strictest moral sense, the cause of the event; and it is justly imputed to him, whatever physical causes may have concurred in its production. (EAP I.vii: 40)

If Reid is right about this, we should distinguish an agent's being the cause of the actualization of a behavior-state from an agent's being a cause "in the strictest moral sense" of an actualization of a behavior-state.

It will be helpful to get a firmer grip on this distinction. Let's say that an agent is the *pure cause* of the actualization of a behavior-state B when and only when she is the sole agent cause of the actualization of B. When an agent is the pure cause of the actualization of a behavior state, then the actualization of that behavior-state is an action in the narrow sense; it is exertion of active power or the formation or enaction of a volition. In contrast, let's say that an agent is a *moral cause* of the actualization of B when and only when she is *an* agent cause (though not necessarily the only agent cause) of B and can rightly be held accountable for the actualization of B. When an agent is a moral cause of the actualization of a behavior-state, then the actualization of that behavior-state is an action in either the narrow or wide sense. So the action could be either something such as deciding to throw a baseball through a window or throwing it through a window. Reid tells us that we are often the moral causes of actions in the wide sense. This is because agents know by experience that exerting their active power is ordinarily accompanied by movements of their bodies and events in the world that are linked by natural laws to these bodily movements.

What we've learned is that Reid operates with two understandings of action (narrow and wide) and two understandings of what it is to be a cause of action (pure and moral). There is an additional layer of complexity of which to take note. For Reid also acknowledges that actions can be ascribed to agents to different *degrees*. Developing a common trope that pits reason against the passions, Reid writes that ordinary people

> have considered this cool principle [i.e., reason], as having an influence upon our actions so different from passion, that what a man does coolly and deliberately, without passion, is imputed solely to the man, whether it have merit or demerit; whereas, what he does from passion is imputed in part to the passion. If the passion be conceived to be irresistible, the action is imputed solely to it, and not at all to the man. If he had power to resist, and ought to have resisted, we blame him for not doing his duty; but, in proportion to the violence of the passion, the fault is alleviated. (EAP II.ii: 56; *cp.* 58–9)

Reid is thus led to embrace a position according to which actions are often partially ascribed to agents. Reid's thinking is that doing so helps to make sense of the phenomenon of holding agents partially accountable for what they do. In Reid's view, then, there is a correlation between the degree to which an action can be ascribed to an agent and the degree to which she is responsible. Roughly, the degree to which the actualization of a behavior-state is your action is the degree to which you are responsible for the actualization of that behavior-state.[36]

But there is no simple correspondence here. When it comes to responsibility, things are messier than that. To see why, consider a case in which an agent's anger produces in him a behavior-state, such as blurting some hurtful words. Imagine that the agent is responsible to a high degree for the actualization of the behavior-state because he could have readily exercised self-command to prevent it. In this case, the agent is responsible to a high degree for blurting these words. But, under Reid's view, the degree of responsibility fails to correspond to the degree to which the actualization of the behavior-state is that agent's action. After all, the blurting is not produced through the agent's exertion of active power; it is produced by a nonvoluntary affective state – namely, the agent's anger. Under Reid's view, then, the blurting is not that agent's action in either the narrow or the wide sense. It follows that, under Reid's view, it is possible for

---

[36] Elsewhere, Reid introduces further complications, noting that degree of willpower bears upon our evaluation of action: "Thus we see, that the power which we are led by common sense to ascribe to man, respects his voluntary actions only, and that it has various limitations even with regard to them. Some actions that depend upon our will are easy, others very difficult, and some perhaps, beyond our power. In different men, the power of self-government is different, and in the same man at different times. It may be diminished, or perhaps lost, by bad habits; it may be greatly increased by good habits" (EAP IV.vi: 235).

there to be cases in which you are responsible to a high degree for the actualization of a behavior-state, but it is false that that actualization is your action. The degree of responsibility for an action, then, is sometimes determined by other factors, such as whether you could have exerted active power to prevent the actualization of a behavior-state and how easily you could have done so. Otherwise put, the degree of responsibility for an action is determined by the degree of *control* that you have over the actualization of your behavior-states.

We have been exploring how Reid understands action. The interpretation at which we've arrived is that Reid uses the term "action" in different ways: sometimes he has action in the narrow sense in mind, while other times he has action in the wide sense in mind. We can be held accountable not only for actions of both sorts but also for the actualization of behavior-states that are not actions but over which we can exercise control. Distinguishing different types of action, as Reid appears to do, has the disadvantage of multiplying senses of "action." But the disadvantage might be only apparent. Reid is happy to allow that one and the same term expresses a multiplicity of meanings provided that such an allowance is justified. And in this case, it looks as if it may be. Given certain theoretical purposes in which we are attempting to identify, in a philosophically precise way, what counts as an action (and, hence, a free action), we need to operate with the narrow understanding of action. But, given certain practical purposes in which we engage in practices of holding each other accountable for what we do, we need to employ the wide understanding of action. In fact, we've seen that Reid's considered view seems to be more expansive than this. We also need to employ the notion of agential control, because we can hold agents responsible for the actualization of behavior-states that are not actions (in Reid's senses of the term). If Reid is right, we need to employ multiple action and behavior concepts in order to serve this range of purposes. His discussion reflects a sensitivity to these different contexts.

2.2 Motives

Reid's discussion of motives parallels his discussion of action. For a close reading of the *Active Powers* reveals that just as Reid operates with two different understandings of action, he also works with two different understandings of motives. The position Reid presents in the early chapter "On the Influence of Incitements and Motives on the Will" is what I will call the *wide understanding of motives*. It says that motives come in two sorts: some are mental states (such as beliefs and desires), while others are the objects of those

mental states—the ends for which agents act (EAP II.ii). Reid affirms that
motives of both sorts contribute to action, but only mental states are *producers*
of action. The view of motives Reid presents in the later chapter "Of the
Influence of Motives" is what I'll label the *narrow understanding of motives*.
It says that motives come in only one sort: those ends for the sake of which an
agent acts (EAP IV.iv). Under this view, motives contribute to but are not
producers of action. We'll see that these two understandings of motives not
only are different but also do not appear easily reconcilable.

Let us have a closer look at each approach, beginning with the wide understanding of motives. In the previous subsection, we noted that Reid distinguishes among the mechanical, animal, and rational principles of action. This
three-part categorization makes sense under the wide understanding of motives.
The mechanical and animal principles are naturally characterized as mental
states that push us to action, while the rational motives are the ends for the sake
of which we act.[37] The wide understanding of motives incorporates all three
types of principle, denominating each a type of motive (*cf.* EAP II.ii). It is more
difficult to make sense of Reid's three-part characterization under the narrow
understanding of motives. For according to the narrow account, the only
motives are ends and, so, include only the rational principles of action.
According to this view, whatever contribution the mechanical and animal
principles make to action, it is not that of being a motive. They are probably
better labeled (to use Reid's own terminology) "incitements."

Let me clarify what Reid means when he speaks of motives as ends, as his
presentation conceals complexity worth making explicit. What Reid calls
"ends" come in two kinds. Ends of the first sort are what I'll call *agent-
reasons*. To acquaint yourself with this concept, think of some case in which
you perform an action and the consideration in light of which you performed
that action. Suppose, for example, that you pruned your apple trees last week.
Although this is a somewhat tedious job, you have done it because your local
arborist has recommended that you do so. The fact that an expert, the arborist,
has recommended that you prune your apple trees is what (in your estimation)
made the action worth performing or recommended its performance. It is the
consideration in light of which you have pruned your trees, your agent-reason.
Under a natural interpretation, Reid holds that the rational principles of action
are among our agent-reasons. Ends of the second sort are what I will call *end-
states*. These are states that an agent endeavors to actualize through the exertion
of his active power. Examples of end-states would be your pruning an apple tree

---

[37] Although, see EAP V.vii: 360, where Reid writes that the mechanical and animal principles are
    ultimate ends. I think Reid must be speaking loosely here.

or kicking a ball into the left-hand corner of a goal. They are not what favor the actualization of a behavior-state but are the behavior-states whose actualization is favored.

Ends of both sorts play a role in action. Agents act to bring about end-states in light of agent-reasons. Somewhat more exactly, Reid's view is that, cases of indifferent action aside, an agent acts for the sake of an end if and only if there is some end-state E such that that agent actualizes E through the exertion of her active power in light of some agent-reason R. In the next section, it will become increasingly apparent why it is worth marking the distinction between different kinds of ends. For now let me simply note that doing so enables us to prevent a certain type of misunderstanding. Reid often says that the rational principles of action are ends. One might be tempted to infer that he believes that they are that for the sake of which we act. For example, one might be tempted to infer that because Reid believes that the principle of duty is an end, we often act for the sake of duty. But he typically does not mean this. Rather, Reid means that the rational principles of action are those in light of which we act and which we take to favor actions, such as helping those in distress and distributing goods equitably. (I hasten to add that the distinction between agent-reasons and end-states is compatible with there being cases in which an agent's agent-reasons for acting are identical with the end-states she endeavors to actualize.)

I've suggested that Reid works with two incompatible views regarding the character of motives—the wide and the narrow understandings. What is perhaps most troubling is that neither view seems well-suited to Reid's purposes. The problem with the narrow understanding is that it would exclude incitements such as desires and passions from playing a productive role in action. But these states certainly *seem* to play such a role in action, as the sentimentalists recognized. The problem with the wide understanding is that if incitements were to play a productive role in action, they would be (what Reid calls) the physical causes of action. Remember, though, that Reid commits himself to the claim that all causality is really agent causality. It follows that were a desire a physical cause of your action, it would typically be the effect of the exertion of someone else's active power—presumably, God's—on you.[38] This poses a threat to Reid's account of action. For Reid's view is that when you act—and, hence, act freely—that action consists not in the exertion of some other agent's active power but in the exertion of *your* active power. So it looks as if Reid must hold that when you act, your act has one and only one agent cause: you.[39]

---

[38] I add the qualifier "typically" because there may be some desires that agents intentionally bring about in themselves through the exertion of active power. But Reid does not treat these as the typical or the paradigm case.

[39] See Yaffe (2004, 44).

We have before us the materials for the following dilemma:

(1*) If the narrow understanding of motives is true, then incitements have no motivational role to play in the production of action. For, if they did, actions would have too many causes. (and, so, could not be free)

(2*) If the wide understanding of motives is true, then the actualizations of behavior-states that Reid maintains are paradigmatic actions, such as pruning apple trees and flagging down cabs, are not actions at all, as they would have too many causes. (and, so, could not be free)

So,

If either the narrow or the wide understanding of motives is true, then incitements have no motivational role to play in the production of action, or the actualizations of behavior-states that Reid maintains are paradigmatic actions are not actions at all.

Both options look unattractive.

Nowhere in the *Active Powers* does Reid offer any suggestions about how to reconcile the different things he says about motives. But there might be resources within his thought that enable him to do so.[40]

As we've seen, in Reid's view, an agent can be more or less responsible for an action, depending (inter alia) to what degree that action is the product of an incitement (EAP I.vii: 40). Roughly, the greater the degree to which an action is the product of an incitement, the less responsible the agent is for performing that action. This suggests that Reid was (at times) comfortable with the idea that actions can have multiple causes. And if actions can have multiple causes, then it would be possible for the actualization of a behavior-state to count as an agent's action, even though it has multiple causes.

According to our earlier discussion, one test for whether the actualization of a behavior-state counts as an agent's action is whether the agent is a moral cause of the actualization of that behavior-state: she is an agent cause of the action and can rightly be held accountable (to some degree) for it. If she is a moral cause, then the actualization of a behavior-state counts as that agent's action (in at least the wide sense). Because Reid does seem willing to countenance cases in which agents are the moral cause of the actualization of a behavior-state and in which that actualization has multiple causes, it looks as if Reid can reject premise (2*) of the objection stated above. That is, he can deny the claim that what appear to be paradigmatic actions, such as pruning apple trees and flagging down cabs, are not actions at all, because they would have too many causes. Of course, this maneuver would require Reid to reject the claim that actions can have one and

---

[40] Cuneo (2011) provides further discussion.

only one agent cause. But for the reasons just given, there are grounds to believe that Reid is already committed to its rejection, independently of the dilemma that we have identified. Under this reading, Reid's considered view is as follows. According to the narrow understanding of action, actions can have one and only one agent cause, namely, the agent herself. But under the wide understanding, they can have multiple agent causes, which include other agents.

We saw earlier that Reid's decision to work with different conceptions of action appears not to be haphazard. Some conceptions appear suitable for certain theoretical purposes, while others do not. Something similar seems to be true of Reid's decision to work with different conceptions of motives. In fact, we are now positioned to see at least this pattern in Reid's thought: the narrow account of motives, according to which the only motives are ends, fits well with the narrow understanding of action. It enables Reid to explain how agents can at once act in light of motives and be the pure cause of their volitions. The wide account of motives, according to which motives can be mental states or ends, fits comfortably with the wide understanding of action. For this understanding of action, we've seen, is compatible with actions having multiple causes. It is worth observing that the wide understanding of motives also fits well with Reid's idea that we can hold agents responsible for behavior-states that are not actions but whose actualizations are nonetheless under their control.

2.3 Active Power

Puzzling through what Reid says about action and motives requires exegetical work. Yet things get only more vexed when we turn to what Reid says about active power. Addressing the topic is unavoidable, however, if we wish to understand Reid's views, because so much of what Reid says turns on the notion of active power. It is, after all, Reid's commitment to our having active power that compels him to work with the narrow views of both action and motives. These views of both action and motives are, as it were, tailored to fit Reid's agent-causal understanding of action. I want here to have a closer look at what Reid says about active power. My primary aim is not to slice through the puzzling features of what Reid says in order to arrive at and defend a compelling interpretation of Reid's views.[41] It will be enough simply to get a clearer sense of what exactly Reid commits himself to when he says that agents, who are endowed with active power, are the causes of their actions and to gesture toward an understanding of Reid's views that strikes me as promising.

The standard interpretation of Reid is that he commits himself to the "classical" account of agent causation according to which agents bear a unique

---

[41] Cuneo and Harp (2019) address the issues in more detail.

irreducible sort of causal relation to their volitions or actions – namely, the agent-causal relation.[42] According to the classical account, perspicuous renderings of causal statements involving agents take the form of expressions such as "A causes E" or "A stands in the agent-causal relation to E"—where "A" stands for an agent (or substance) and "E" stands for an event. Philosophers have long held that the classical account is vulnerable to a battery of objections. Some charge that it leads to a vicious infinite regress of agent-causings. Others allege that the view cannot accomplish the work Reid and others want it to; it fails to explain how we could act freely. Still others find the view exceedingly strange.[43]

As indicated, I am not going to address these concerns directly (although our discussion will bear upon them in some important ways). I will, however, make one remark about a type of concern that is sometimes raised regarding views such as Reid's (and perhaps lies behind the charge that the view is strange). The concern is that countenancing two sorts of causal relations, event and agent-causal relations, is theoretically ungainly. To the extent that advocates of agent causation embrace both species of causation, their views are less streamlined than they ought to be. The charge fails to stick to Reid's view. For we have seen that, strictly speaking, Reid denies that event (or so-called physical) causation is a kind of causation distinct from agent (or efficient) causation. In Reid's view, there is only one sort of causation. That is what he calls "efficient" causation and what we have been calling agent causation. That noted, let us now pursue the question of whether the standard interpretation is correct to attribute the classical view to Reid. I believe there is reason to think it is not.

Begin with a range of texts in which Reid clearly states what he has in mind by a cause:

> That which produces a change by the exertion of its power, we call the *cause* of that change; and the change produced, the *effect* of that cause. (EAP I.i: 13)

> I consider the determination of the will as an effect. This effect must have a cause which had power to produce it; and the cause must be either the person himself, whose will it is, or some other being. (EAP IV.i: 201)

> The name of a *cause* and of an agent, is properly given to that being only, which by its active power, produces some change in itself, or in some other being. (EAP 268)

> In the strict and proper sense, I take an efficient cause to be a being who had power to produce the effect, and exerted that power for that purpose. (Cor 174)

---

[42] See, among others, Kane (2005, 5.4), Lowe (2008, 151n9), O'Connor (1994), Van Cleve (2015, ch. 15), and Yaffe (2004).

[43] Chisholm (2003) and Van Cleve (2015, ch. 15) raise (and address) the first worry; van Inwagen (2017, introduction) raises the second; Taylor (1974) broaches the third.

> I think we agree in this, that a cause, in the proper and strict sense ... signifies a being or mind that has power and will to produce the effect. (Cor 178; *cf.* OP 6)

In addition, consider a text in which Reid clearly specifies the conditions under which an agent stands in the causal relation to an effect:

> In order to the production of any effect, there must be in the cause, not only power, but the exertion of that power: For power that is not exerted produces no effect. All that is necessary to the production of any effect, is power in an efficient cause to produce the effect, and the exertion of that power. (EAP IV.ii: 268)

Let us call the first group of passages the "agent-cause texts" and the second, individual passage "the exertion text."[44] Two observations about these passages are in order.

The first is that in the agent-cause texts, Reid explicitly says that a cause is an agent or mind. But nowhere does Reid explicitly commit himself to there being an agent-causal relation in which agents stand to events. Rather, Reid merely commits himself to:

> Necessarily, every action A has an agent cause.

But this claim does not imply:

> Necessarily, every action A is such that there is an agent cause to which A bears the agent-causal relation.

Perhaps the easiest way to see why the implication fails to hold is to consider a view of the following sort.

Suppose, first, that agents instantiate active power. In the passages just quoted, this is the sense in which Reid says they are causes. Suppose, second, that when agents recognize a strong reason to act, their active power is activated thereby (at least provided that a variety of enabling conditions hold). Note that a view such as this endorses the claim that every action has an agent cause: when an agent acts, that agent is the bearer or ground of the activation of active power. But the view does not imply that when an agent acts, that agent bears some irreducible agent-causal relation to that action, as the standard interpretation avers. To the contrary, the position sketched simply involves an agent being the ground of active power and that power's being activated by that agent's awareness of reasons (in conjunction with a variety of other enabling conditions). Given the plausible

---

[44] It is important to emphasize that while Reid holds that everything with active power must have a will, he distinguishes active power from will; see EAP I.v: 32. So, in Reid's view, active power is both different from and more fundamental than will, and is necessarily exerted when we will: "By the *liberty* of a moral agent, I understand, a power over the determination of his own will" (EAP IV.i: 267; *cp.* Cor 130–33, OP 4).

assumption that the agent-causal relation is not reducible to an agent's being the ground of active power in conjunction with that power's being activated, it follows that an action's having an agent cause does not imply that agents bear an irreducible agent-causal relation to their actions.

The first observation I've made is that what Reid says about agent (or "efficient") causes does not support the standard interpretation of Reid's view according to which agents bear an irreducible agent-causal relation to their actions. The second observation I'd like to make concerns how we might harmonize what Reid says in the exertion text—which says that the production of an effect includes *both* active power and its exertion—with the standard interpretation. Their harmonization, I want to suggest, is not easily achieved. Consider the following three interpretive options.

The first option proposes that the agent-causal relation wholly consists in the exertion of active power. In that case, the first relatum of this relation is not a substance. It is the exertion of active power, which, by all appearances, is an event. So under this interpretation, the agent-causal relation looks as if it obtains between the exertion of active power (an event) and the formation (or enactment) of volition (also an event). That, however, is incompatible with the classical view, which holds that the agent-causal relation holds between a substance and an event.

The second option proposes that the agent-causal relation wholly consists in the exertion of active power but that, despite appearances, any such exertion is *not* an event. To say that an agent exerted active power is just a way of speaking about an agent's being such that she stands in the agent-causal relation to some volition. While the proposal might be coherent, it is difficult to see how it could be principled. It looks as if Reid would have to commit himself to the view that what look like paradigm events or happenings are not events at all.[45]

Unlike the first option, the third option rejects the idea that the agent-causal relation wholly consists in the exertion of active power. Instead, it proposes that when agents act, there are two relations present: an event-causal relation, which consists in the exertion of active power, and an irreducible agent-causal relation. The problem with this option is that it posits too many types of causes. In order to explain action, one type of cause should suffice.

In short, there appear to be two challenges facing the standard interpretation. It does not look as if there is textual evidence to support it. That is, it does not look as if there are texts in which Reid asserts or implies that when agents act, they stand in an irreducible agent-causal relation to their volitions. To the contrary, the agent-cause texts appear only to support the more modest claim

---

[45] I understand Rowe (1991) and O'Connor (1994) to commit Reid to something like this option.

that every act must have an agent (efficient) cause. Second, the standard interpretation does not sit well with the exertion text. Attributing the classical view to Reid subjects his position to what appear to be some fairly imposing conceptual challenges. While I think it is fair to say that any position in this vicinity will face some serious challenges, it is worth asking whether these are the challenges that Reid's view faces.

I suspect they are not. A helpful way to approach the issues is by having before us two positions regarding action explanation that Reid rejects but whose insights he incorporates into his own view. On the one side are purely teleological views. These positions endeavor to explain action purely by reference to the end-states that agents endeavor to actualize, and the agent-reasons in light of which they act.[46] When it comes to action explanation, causality does not enter into the picture. On the other side are purely causal views. These positions attempt to explain action solely by reference to the causal roles played by mental states, such as beliefs and desires.[47] Agent-reasons do not enter the picture. Reid's position incorporates commitments from each of these views.

The Reidian position agrees with teleological views in this sense: any satisfactory explanation of action must advert to the end-states an agent endeavors to actualize and the agent-reasons in light of which an agent acts. That, in large measure, is why Reid characterizes motives as he does. Motives, understood in the narrow sense, must be not what produce action but what contribute in a noncausal way to the explanation of action.[48] But Reid does not present this as the entire explanatory story with regard to action explanation. There is also a causal dimension to action. In Reid's view, the primary causal contributor to action is not a type of mental state, such as a belief or a desire, but the exertion of active power. As the passages above reveal, Reid will sometimes write that a cause is that which, *by* the exertion of its power, produces some change. I suspect Reid's use of the "by" locution is misleading. It suggests that there is something the agent does that eventuates in the exertion of active power. That cannot, however, be Reid's view (at least if he wishes to avoid a vicious regress of exertions of active power). It is better to say that the agent produces some change *through* the exertion of active power. That is compatible with there being nothing that the agent does in order to exert active power.

I believe this to be Reid's considered view. Agents are causes, and through the exertion of active power, they form and enact volitions. But there is nothing an agent does in order to exert active power. Call this interpretation the *networked-*

---

[46] Recent defenses of the view include Sehon (2005) and (2016).
[47] Davidson (1980) is the most famous contemporary proponent of this view.
[48] "The relation between motives and actions is totally of a different kind from that which physical causes bear to their effects" (Cor 179).

capacity view. The name is apt because it tells us that what it is to be an agent is to be the seat of a network of capacities, including reason, active power, and will.[49] These capacities stand in a complex, unified network of relations. Active power is sensitive to the deliverances of reason, which include the presentation of end-states and agent-reasons. It is exerted for the sake of actualizing such end-states and in light of the agent-reasons presented. Active power, in turn, is linked to the will in such a way that when it is exerted, volitions are formed. It should be added that whether active power is exerted on some occasion will depend not simply on whether there is an end-state and an agent-reason that an agent grasps. As Reid indicates, it will depend instead on a whole host of contextual factors, such as the character of the reason grasped (e.g., whether it is decisive or recommending), how it is grasped (e.g., clearly or hazily), the agent's concerns (e.g., whether she cares about performing acts of a particular kind), her dispositions (e.g., whether she is the sort of person who has resolved to act on reasons of this sort), and so on (cf. EAP II.iii; III.iv: 220 and IIII.iii. viii). Any reasonably accurate and detailed explanation of why an agent acts on some occasion will be complex.

According to the networked-capacity view, when an agent acts, there is nothing the agent does to exert active power. Exertions of active power are instead uncaused, basic actions and, so, "causally spontaneous."[50] Would this interpretation satisfactorily account for the fact that when action occurs, it is *agents* who act and not merely their powers that are actualized? After all, it is not difficult to imagine a scenario in which you are endowed with a power that spontaneously exerts itself but you do not experience these exertions as your actions.

The worry just raised strikes me as genuine. I think a satisfactory answer would have to emphasize two things. I close by presenting them.

The first can be captured by the slogan "Agency (necessarily) comes with perspective." The idea here is that agents bear a very close relation to active power, will, and reason: they are essentially constituted by this network of capacities. As such, Reid must hold that the intimacy of this relation involves agents having a perspective on their own behavior that necessarily involves experiencing the exertion of active power *as* their acting.[51] The perspective is

---

[49] See note 44 regarding Reid's distinction between active power and will.

[50] I borrow the term "spontaneous" from Lowe (2008, ch. 8), who compares the power of the will to that of radium atoms whose activation is also uncaused.

[51] Reid may gesture at this idea when he writes: "As I am unable to form a notion of any intellectual power different in kind from those I possess, the same holds with respect to active power . . . In like manner, if he had not some degree of active power, and if he were not conscious of the exertion of it in his voluntary actions, it is probable he could have no conception of activity, or of active power" (EAP I.V: 30).

not like the one we have regarding our own digestive processes; it is not the perspective in which we recognize that some process is happening to or in us that is uniquely ours. Rather, it is the first-person, agential perspective of doing something. The perspective I have on the exertion of my active power is that *I*, the agent, am doing something. Reid must be presupposing that this perspective is essential to being the subject of the networked capacities of active power, will, and reason. It is essentially constitutive of active power so understood that an agent experiences its exertions as *her* exertions. It would be one of Kant's signal contributions to call attention to this presupposition, which is part of what he calls the unity of apperception.

Reid gestures at why having this perspective is essential to having active power when he writes,

> It is of the highest importance to us, as moral and accountable creatures, to know what actions are in our power, because it is for these only that we can be accountable to our Maker, or to our fellow-men in society; by these only we can merit praise or blame; in these only all our prudence, wisdom, and virtue must be employed; and, therefore, with regard to them, the wise Author of nature has not left us in the dark. (EAP I.v: 30)

The thinking seems to be this: we can be accountable for our actions only if we know which actions are ours. Suppose, however, active power were such that we did not experience its exertions as an exercise of our own agency. That is, suppose we were to experience it as a power that while grounded in our being, spontaneously exerts itself. Under these conditions, we would not know which actions are ours. After all, we might reasonably attribute agency to the spontaneous exertions of active power itself. But because we are accountable, we know that the exertions of active powers are our actions. We can know that they are our actions, however, only if we experience them as such. So an agent must bear the agential perspective to the exercise of her active power.

The second thing to say, which Reid emphasizes in his late essay "On Power," is that this unique first-personal perspective on the exertion of active power is often accompanied by a distinct, albeit difficult-to-characterize phenomenology. This phenomenology is often that of *trying* to do or accomplish something. Reid draws attention to this phenomenology when he writes that we "are conscious of many voluntary exertions, some easy, others more difficult, some requiring a great effort. These are exertions of power" (EAP IV.vi: 229; *cf.* EAP OP 5). Again, the experience is not that of there being something that is occurring within me that requires great effort; it is rather that this effort of mine requires resolve and considerable concentration. What should be added is that, in Reid's view, the perspective and its accompanying phenomenology are not illusory. They reveal the way things are.

2.4 Conclusion

Agency-centered approaches to ethical theorizing require us to identify the relations that hold between agency, on the one hand, and ethical action and evaluation, on the other. In this section, we've focused on what Reid says about agency and how it intersects with action, motivation, and active power. What Reid says about these issues is perplexing. He does not explicitly state that he is using terms such as "action" and "motive" in multiple ways or why he would do so. Moreover, his discussion of the agent as cause is liable to be understood in ways that, I suspect, do not reflect Reid's own views. Still, there are ways of making sense of what Reid says on these topics.

The key to understanding what Reid says about action and motives, I've suggested, is to appreciate the degree to which Reid is willing to allow his discussion to be shaped by different concerns. One concern is to speak in philosophically precise ways that make sense of the claim that we are free. Another concern is to make sense of ordinary ascriptions of responsibility. According to the interpretation I've offered, the best way to understand Reid's approach is to appreciate that the terms "action" and "motive" can be said in many ways.

Unpacking Reid's claim that agents are causes proves to be even more challenging. The standard interpretation has been to ascribe to Reid a view according to which, when agents act, they bear an irreducible agent-causal relation to their action. I have argued that what Reid says does not support this interpretation. I have presented, as an alternative, the networked-capacity position, according to which agents are essentially constituted by a network of capacities that play different roles in action. Active power plays a unique role in the sense that it is the executive practical capacity through the exercise of which agents act.

3 Two Challenges

We have been engaged in two primary tasks. The first has been to understand the role of the rational principles of action in normative governance. This has helped us to trace some of the contours of Reid's agency-centered approach. The second has been to work through what Reid says about action, motives, and active power. That has enabled us to better understand some puzzling elements of Reid's view of agency. It has also provided materials for an enriched understanding of normative governance. We have learned that engaging in normative governance involves employing the rational principles of action in order to manage one's motives and native capacities. While many of the details need to be filled in, we now have a better understanding of the types of motives and types of action that can be involved in such governance, and the agent's role in such management.

This section broadens the discussion by engaging with Reid's metaethical views. Its aim is to illustrate some ways in which Reid's broadly rational intuitionist commitments intersect with what he says about the rational principle of action, on the one hand, and motives and agency, on the other. So I will be picking up on elements of our discussion in the previous two sections, albeit by bringing them into conversation with Reid's metaethics. I frame the discussion by considering two challenges to Reid's position, which press it from different directions.

The first challenge is typically voiced by those sympathetic with broadly naturalistic, Aristotelian approaches; the second has its home in the sentimentalist tradition. While Reid would have been familiar with the philosophical convictions that drive these objections, he himself addresses neither challenge explicitly. I believe it will be fruitful to consider them. After all, posing objections to historical figures often reveals nuances and tensions within their views of which they were unaware. Moreover, it sometimes reveals the resources a figure might have to help resolve them. And that, in turn, can help us deepen our understanding of that figure's views. Let me add that I have not picked these challenges from thin air. They have been offered as reasons for rejecting positions such as Reid's. While satisfactory answers to these challenges would probably have to go considerably beyond anything that Reid says or what is said here, it should be instructive both to identify what types of answers are available to Reid and what else would need to be said in order to supplement them.

3.1 The Aristotelian Objection

The first challenge, which I'll call the Aristotelian Objection, runs as follows:

> A satisfactory ethical theory must be embedded within and comport with
> a substantive and informative account of human nature and the good (telos)
> for human beings. For only this will enable us to both gain a sufficiently

comprehensive view of the ethical domain, and to address pressing questions, such as why we should be virtuous. Reid's view is a species of rational intuitionism. According to rational intuitionist views, however, moral reality has nothing essentially to do with human nature or the good (telos) for human beings. What we morally ought to do, for example, is not grounded in what fulfills our nature. Instead, rational intuitionism tells us that moral truths are like mathematical truths. They exist and are graspable but are independent of us in just about every interesting sense. Since moral reality has nothing essentially to do with human nature or the good for human beings, questions about what makes acts right or traits virtuous are closed-off, as these questions essentially appeal to what sort of beings we are. There is nothing to say about these ethical properties other than they exist and we grasp them by intuition. Moreover, there is the additional worry that in comparing the moral domain to the mathematical one, rational intuitionists misdescribe the character of that with which ethical theorizing concerns itself. Far from being a theoretical domain such as mathematics, which concerns itself only with what we are to believe, morality is fundamentally a practical domain that primarily concerns itself with how we should act.

Given rational intuitionism's shortcomings, our best bet is to look elsewhere when engaging in ethical theorizing. Specifically, we should look backward to the views of the ancients and medievals (perhaps suitably amended or qualified) for views that are not susceptible to these failings. For, contrary to rational intuitionism, the views of the ancients and medievals are developed within a rich account of what human beings are and what their good (telos) consists in.[52]

It may be worth adding that some philosophers, such as Bernard Williams, endorse this line of criticism but reject the proposed solution. According to Williams, a return to the teleology of the ancients and medievals is untenable.[53] If he is correct, we should draw a skeptical verdict from the Aristotelian Objection. We should embrace neither rational intuitionism nor the views of the ancients and the medievals. We must instead radically reconceive the subject matter of ethics.

One reason I am interested in exploring the Aristotelian Objection is that I believe Reid would take it seriously. While he could be critical of his predecessors, Reid was also at pains to emphasize that he didn't take himself to engage in innovative ethical theorizing. Instead, he was eager to connect his own views with those of Plato, Aristotle, and especially the Stoics, proclaiming at points that he was not saying "any thing that is new, but what reason suggested to those who first turned their attention to the philosophy of morals" (EAP III.iii.ii: 155).[54]

---

[52] Irwin (2006, 808–10) and MacIntyre (1984, 55, 59, 64–5) and (1990, ch. 8) articulate versions of this challenge. Heydt (2018) contextualizes the disagreement between Aristotelianism and the broadly Pufendorfian position endorsed by figures such as Reid.

[53] See Williams (1985).

[54] Compare Sidgwick (1907), who dismisses Plato and Aristotle as producing "sham-axioms" and the Stoic system as a "complicated enchainment of circular reasonings." The passage is quoted in Hurka (2014, 259).

Moreover, as I've emphasized, Reid assumes that ethical theorizing must be done within the context of a substantive account of agency. The charge that in actuality, his view floats free of human nature would be unwelcome.

The Aristotelian Objection makes several claims that seem correct. Reid's position does incorporate rational intuitionist commitments. It implies that we noninferentially grasp moral propositions via conscience or the moral sense, which is a dimension of practical reason. It also (favorably) compares morals to math. Paradigm moral truths are claimed to be necessary and self-evident, just as mathematical ones are (cf. EIP VII.ii). Finally, like most rational intuitionist views, Reid's position rejects the eudaimonism of the ancients and medievals (see §1.2). While these claims accurately describe Reid's view, there is reason to believe that the Aristotelian Objection does not hit the mark.

I think the best way to explain why is to begin with Reid's methodology. In section 1, I developed the claim that it would be misleading to characterize Reid's methodology as that of common sense. It is more diverse than that. Still, what Reid has to say about the first principles of morals leans heavily on a commonsense methodology, which I'll call a *content-first* approach. It instructs theorists to engage in three activities.

The first is to extract from ordinary moral thought and practice general moral principles that plain persons must take for granted in their everyday lives on pain of there being reason to believe that they suffer from a deficiency such as insincerity, conceptual incompetence, insanity, or the like. These general moral principles are what Reid calls the first principles of morals. Recall they include standards such as:

> It is prima facie wrong to wound, maim, or kill others.
> It is prima facie wrong to destroy the reputation of others.
> It is prima facie wrong to break our promises to others.

The second task is to grant pride of place to these principles, treating them as having considerable (albeit defeasible) evidential weight when theorizing.[55] Reid calls attention to this aspect of his methodology late in the *Active Powers*. After having noted that conflicting moral theories often agree about first-order moral principles, Reid writes,

> From this remarkable disparity between our decisions in the theory of morals and in the rules of morality, we may, I think, draw this conclusion, that wherever we find any disagreement between the practical rules of morality, which have been received in all ages, and the principles of any of the theories

---

[55] One can find Reid's comments regarding the defeasible character of first principles at EIP I.i: 26–7; *cp.* Wolterstorff (2004, 99–100).

advanced upon this subject, the practical rules ought to be the standard by
which the theory is to be corrected. (EAP V.iv: 290–1)[56]

Principles such as these, Reid continues, "serve as a touchstone" for assessing
a variety of ethical theories (EAP V.iv: 290).

The third task is to conduct one's theorizing in such a way that it incorporates
the relevant principles, ensuring that it is compatible with whatever other
principles of common sense there may be. In principle, there are a variety of
ways to do so. Reid does so by incorporating the first principles of morals into
a pluralist, deontological ethical theory.[57]

Let me now make explicit how Reid's content-first approach bears upon the
Aristotelian Objection. I begin by offering a diagnosis. The Aristotelian
Objection correctly states that, according to Reid,

> (A) The first principles of morals are necessary, self-evident moral standards.
> Because they are self-evident, they cannot be derived from principles more
> evident.

It then moves to the claim that, according to Reid,

> (B) The first principles of morals do not admit of direct defense or explan-
> ation. Among other things, they cannot be grounded in facts regarding human
> nature or the human good, such as facts that concern what fulfills human
> nature or achieves the human good.

The objection concludes by claiming that, under Reid's view, the first principles
of morals float free from facts involving human nature or the human good much
in the way that the axioms of arithmetic do.[58]

Reid would rightly point out that both steps in the objection are problematic.
Begin with the move from (A) to (B). Note that (A) is compatible with there being
propositions from which we can derive and explain the first principles of morals.
(A) simply rules out the possibility that any such proposition is more evident than
the first principles of morals themselves. When speaking carefully, Reid acknowledges this (EIP I.ii: 39). Admittedly, deriving a first principle from some
proposition that is no more evident than that principle itself may not enhance its
epistemic status.[59] Indeed, in one place, Reid worries that any such derivation
may have the effect of making first principles seem less evident than they are

---

[56] Reid reiterates the point at EAP V.iv: 290.
[57] Some passages suggest that Reid takes this approach a step further, embracing a view according
to which the acceptance of the first principles is *constitutive* of moral thought; *cp*. EIP VII.ii: 723,
and EAP III.iii. vi: 234, IV.vii: 239. Cuneo (2014) explores the issue.
[58] See Irwin (2006, 808, 810).
[59] I say "may" because such derivations may "boost" the first-principles' epistemic standing in
virtue of exhibiting how they cohere with one another, as Poore (2015) contends.

(EAP V.i: 369). But the worry does not seem to run deep. For elsewhere Reid gestures at a theistic grounding of the first principles of morals, which appeals to the character of the divine essence (EAP V.vii). In countenancing such an explanation, Reid seems to recognize that when constructing theories, we typically do not require that an explanation of the truth of a highly evident proposition *P* must appeal to propositions as evident as *P* itself.

Properly understood, then, claim (A) does not imply claim (B). That noted, Reid seems largely uninterested in providing any explanation why the first principles of morals hold. That is some reason to believe that he regards these principles as being ontologically fundamental, having no grounds. Note, however, that if this is Reid's position, and Reid embraces (B), this would not license the conclusion that the first principles of morals float free of facts concerning human nature or the human good, as the Aristotelian Objection alleges. This is for two reasons.

First, facts regarding human nature can bear upon the first principles of morals by determining their application conditions. Consider positive law as an analogue. What typically grounds a given law are decisions or pronouncements made by qualified parties. But what determines whether such a law applies to someone on some occasion are such things as her legal standing or circumstances. For example, according to US law, every adult who has the standing of being a citizen of the United States has a (defeasible) right to vote.

Unlike legal principles, the first principles of morals, in Reid's view, are not grounded in decisions or pronouncements of any sort. Still, just as there are explanations why legal principles apply to agents of certain kinds, so also are there explanations why moral principles apply to human beings. These explanations involve reference to what sort of things humans are and the circumstances they occupy. In one passage, Reid articulates this idea, writing that the first principles of morals apply to human agents because they have a given nature and occupy certain conditions:

> The propositions which I think are properly called moral, are those that affirm some obligation to be, or not to be incumbent on one or more individual persons ... the subjects [of these propositions] ... are the creatures of God; their obligation results from, the constitution which God has given them, and the circumstances in which he has placed them. That an individual has such a constitution, and is placed in such circumstances, is not an abstract and necessary, but a contingent truth. (EIP 722; *cp.* EAP III.iii.v: 229)

Here Reid's point seems to be that while the first principles of morals hold of necessity, whether they apply to human agents is contingent upon the facts that human agents are endowed with a given constitution, and occupy circumstances of certain kinds.

Facts regarding human nature (or the human good) can bear upon the first principles in a second way, which is revealed when we look inside the principles themselves. Consider the principle

> It is prima facie wrong to break our promises to others.

Under a natural reading, which I believe Reid would endorse, this principle states not just that promise-breakings are wrong but also that promise-breakings *make* actions wrong. That is, this principle is best understood to state

> (C) Necessarily, when an act of promise-breaking is prima facie wrong, it is wrong because it is an act of promise-breaking.

Philosophers often dig deeper, asking why that would be. Some maintain that promise-breakings are wrong because they tend to undercut important elements of human well-being, which have inherent worth, such as relations of trust. Others answer that they involve treating others with disrespect, as having less worth than they in fact possess. Given the assumption that our good on the whole consists in responding appropriately to what has worth and dignity, both answers imply that promise-breakings are prima facie wrong because they involve being inappropriately related to components of our good on the whole.

I have specified two ways in which facts about human nature or the human good bear upon the first principles of morals. If correct, they establish that the latter do not float free of the former, contrary to what claim (B) alleges. It should be conceded, however, that the foregoing probably represents an incomplete response to the Aristotelian Objection. For proponents of the objection will point out that rational intuitionism is naturally understood to claim that the first principles of morals explain why particular acts such as promise-breaking are wrong. The problem is that this answer appears to imply that the wrongness of acts of promise-breaking has too many (full) grounds.

To illustrate, suppose you fail to do as you say on some occasion. According to (C), your act would be prima facie wrong because it is a case of promise-breaking. But if rational intuitionism is correct, your act is wrong because it is a violation of principle (C) itself. But it would be strange if your act were wrong *both* because it is a promise-breaking and a violation of principle (C). One ground should suffice.[60]

Reid does not explicitly address this concern regarding redundancy in grounds. But he appears to have the resources to do so. We can see why by

---

[60] Berker (2019) provides a vivid statement of the worry.

distinguishing robust moral generalizations from moral laws. A *robust moral generalization* is a mere description or summary of how things stand (or must stand) morally. In contrast, a *moral law* explains why things stand (or must stand) in the way they do morally. Under one reading, (C) states a robust moral generalization; it describes an important respect in which promise-breaking and wrongness are related. Reid, however, states that the first principles of morals are not mere generalizations but moral laws (EAP IV.ix: 251; *cp*. V.ii: 280–1). It follows that a more perspicuous rendering of (C) is

> (D) It is a moral law that when an act of promise-breaking is prima facie wrong, it is wrong because it is an act of promise-breaking.

For our purposes, the differences between robust moral generalizations and moral laws are important. Moral generalizations do not ground particular moral facts, but are grounded in them. In contrast, moral laws are not grounded in particular moral facts but ground them in this sense: these laws explain why, necessarily, actions such as promise-breakings ground the fact that they are wrong.[61] Under this reading, Reid's considered view is that principle (D) plays this explanatory role. This view implies no redundancy in grounding, as promise-breakings and (D) ground different things.

If this is correct, Reid can affirm the following four claims:

> The first principles of morals are fundamental: they are not grounded in particular moral facts (or perhaps, in some cases, anything).

> The first principles of morals are explanatory: they explain why both particular moral facts and moral generalizations hold.

> The first principles of morals do not float free of human nature and the good: they specify acts that have a given moral status in virtue of their bearing some relation to aspects of human nature and the human good.

> There is no objectionable redundancy in what fully grounds the moral status of actions. The first principles of morals, understood as laws, are what ultimately do so.

Suppose that the preceding establishes that the first principles of morals do not float free of human nature in the way that, say, the axioms of mathematics appear to. Why would Reid positively compare the two domains, as he does? The Aristotelian Objection charges that the comparison reveals that Reid thinks of the first principles of morals, just like the principles of mathematics, as having nothing to do with human nature. I've argued that this is probably not

---

[61] See Murphy (2011, chs. 1–2) and Rosen (2017, 164), who writes that "proper laws" are "general principles that are not grounded in their instances and which are therefore fit to ground them."

the best reading of Reid. But the question remains why Reid was keen to draw a comparison between the two types of principles.

The content-first approach might shine light on the issue. Charitably understood, the point behind the comparison is not to suggest that moral reality, like mathematical reality, floats free of human nature or the human good. Nor is it to suggest that morality is (or is closely analogous to) a theoretical discipline like mathematics. Reid emphasizes that it isn't (see EAP III.iii.i). Rather, charitably understood, the primary point of the comparison is to suggest that moral and mathematical theorizing have this much in common: the proper way to engage in such theorizing is to employ a content-first strategy. In moral theorizing, there is excellent reason for every moral theory to incorporate the first principles of morals, under a modally robust understanding. In mathematical theorizing, there is excellent reason for a theory to incorporate a variety of first-order mathematical axioms, under a modally robust construal. Moreover, theories of both sorts should acknowledge the highly evident status of these first principles to the plain person. Whether we can explain why these truths hold is, according to this approach, of secondary importance. Were we to pursue such an explanation, as we sometimes should, that explanation must be compatible with and account for the robust modal status of the first principles.

Let me summarize our discussion. The Aristotelian Objection charges that Reid works with an objectionably bifurcated approach to ethical theorizing. On the one hand are the first principles of morals. On the other are human agents. But, the objection charges, Reid fails to explain how the first principles of morals and human nature or the human good bear upon one another. Indeed, because moral reality is not grounded in human nature or the human good, it looks as if there isn't much Reid can say to connect the two. In response, I have contended that the objection fails to make full contact with Reid's views. Reid can explain how human nature and the human good bear upon the first principles of morals, even if these principles are ontologically fundamental. Moreover, I've suggested that Reid's comparison between math and morals has limited import. Still, it should be acknowledged that the Aristotelian Objection is onto something. It rightly points out that Reid is not particularly interested in establishing that the first principles of morals are ultimately grounded in facts involving human nature or the human good.

3.2 The Sentimentalist Objection

I wrote earlier that exploring how a position might respond to a challenge can be instructive because it often brings to light dimensions of a view that we might otherwise not have appreciated. In the previous subsection, I suggested that the

Aristotelian Objection helps us to see dimensions of Reid's view that we might not have noticed. For example, our treatment of the objection helped us to appreciate the centrality of Reid's content-first methodology. In this subsection, I would now like to explore a second challenge, which presses rational intuitionism from a different direction. The main lines of what I'll call the Sentimentalist Objection will be familiar to many.

> Most rational intuitionists affirm a distinction between theoretical reason, which concerns truth, and practical reason, which concerns motivation and action. But in practice, these philosophers have treated practical reason as if it were just a species of theoretical reason in which we grasp abstract moral truths, which resemble mathematical ones, "wafting by."[62] But this way of thinking about practical reason is mistaken. For the deliverances of practical reason, our moral judgments, have a much more intimate connection with motivation and action than they could if practical reason were to be a mere variant of theoretical reason. While rational intuitionists have often affirmed this intimate connection, they have no explanation for it. They do not explain —and it is difficult to see how they could explain—why it would be that cognizing abstract truths would bear such an intimate connection with motivation and action. This is not a minor blemish on the view. As Hume clearly saw, the intimate connection between moral judgment and action is what renders morality what it is, namely, a practical domain. Because rational intuitionists have no explanation for this central feature of the moral domain, we have excellent reason to reject these views and embrace sentimentalist positions, which do explain this intimate connection by appeal to the sentiments.

It is surprising that Reid never explicitly formulates and systematically addresses this objection, especially given that something like it enjoys such prominence in Hume's thinking.[63] But, as we'll see, there is ample textual evidence that Reid was sensitive to the concerns it expresses.

The sentimentalists endorsed a way of thinking about motivation and action that Reid dubbed "the System of Necessity." Central to this view is the following claim about motives:

> For any agent, set of motives M, and action A at t, necessarily, if that agent performs A, then there is some member of M that is that agent's strongest motive, which causes that agent to perform A at t. (*Cp.* EAP IV.iv and IV.ix)

Reid rejects this claim. Actions are not the occurrence of behavior-states occasioned by the strongest motive. Rather, as we saw earlier, actions

---

[62] I borrow the phrase from Korsgaard (1996, 44).

[63] Hume's own misgivings do not, however, appeal to the notion of practical reason; Hutcheson was more comfortable appealing to the notion. See Radcliffe (2018, 212–13).

consist in the exertion of active power. Still, there we noted that Reid works with two different understandings of motives. What I called the wide understanding maintains that motives include both mental states and ends, while the narrow understanding holds that the only motives are ends. Consequently, we find in Reid two rather different and not clearly compatible responses to the Sentimentalist Objection. The first employs the narrow understanding of motives, which appeals only to the rational principles of action, while the second endorses the wide understanding of motives, appealing also to the animal principles of action. I will present each and ask whether they can be harmonized.

Begin with the response that works with the narrow understanding of motives. This response concedes rather little to the Sentimentalist Objection, as it claims that the rational principles of action (or "rational motives") influence the will differently from the animal principles of action (or "animal motives"). Reid explicitly makes this point in the following passage:

> Let us next consider rational motives, to which the name of *motive* is more commonly and more properly given. Their influence is upon the judgment, by convincing that such an action ought to be done, that it is our duty, or conducive to our real good, or to some end which we have determined to pursue.
>
> They do not give a blind impulse to the will as animal motives do. They convince, but they do not impel, unless, as may often happen, they excite some passion of hope, or fear, or desire. Such passions may be excited by conviction, and may operate in its aid as other animal motives do. But there may be conviction without passion; and the conviction of what one ought to do, in order to [achieve] some end which we have judged fit to be pursued, is what I call a *rational motive*. (EAP IV.iv: 218–9; *cp*. EAP II.ii 58–9)

Reid's primary point here is that rational motives do not play a productive role (such as a causal role) in action. Because they are not psychological states but the objects thereof, they cannot trigger the will. Reid underscores the point by noting that rational motives (or "ends") are the wrong sort of thing to trigger the will. They are abstracta and, so, have "no real existence" in space/time (Cor 175; *cp*. EAP IV.iv).

While rational motives do not produce action in the way that psychological states or active power can, they nonetheless play distinctive roles in the production of action. First, they are reasons: that an act is your moral duty favors doing it. They are, second, agent-reasons: you can act in light of the fact that an act is your duty. They are, third, end-states: you can act for the sake of fulfilling your duty, and good agents often do so. Fourth, as the passage above states, they are involved in the generation of affective states: grasping that something is your duty can generate passions such as hope, fear, and desire.[64] And, finally, rational motives play an ineliminable role in action explanation; the explanation of any action taken from rational motives must appeal to them.

It is now apparent how Reid's first response to the Sentimentalist Objection would go. He would accuse the objection as being tendentious. It presupposes a broadly sentimentalist understanding of how motives influence the will according to which they are psychological states that produce action. But that presupposition could not be a compelling reason to believe that the Reidian view assimilates practical reason to theoretical reason. While both practical and theoretical reason have a representational dimension that enable agents to grasp propositions, the entities grasped play very different roles.

The entities grasped by theoretical reason, such as the truths of mathematics or logic, do not as such favor action. Nor are they in themselves agent-reasons, functioning as the favorable light in which agents act. Nor are they end-states that agents endeavor to bring about by the exertion of active power. Nor is their grasp as such intimately involved in the generation of affective states, such as fear, hope, and desire. Nor do they as such play an ineliminable role in action explanation, since actions taken from rational motives needn't appeal to them. In contrast, rational motives, which are grasped by practical reason, play all these roles. As such, they bear a *very* intimate connection with action and, thus, to what renders morality a practical domain. If that is right, it would be inaccurate to accuse a view such as Reid's of somehow omitting a central feature of the moral domain. Rational motives and, so, moral motives, are practical at their core. Now add that the character of practical reason is determined, in part, by what sorts of objects it takes as its inputs, the roles they play, and what it does with these objects, such as employing them in practical deliberation. It follows that, in Reid's view, practical reason is no mere variant of theoretical reason, as the employment of theoretical reason does involve entities playing the roles enumerated above.

Let me add a further point. I have said that Reid's view is deeply indebted to rational intuitionism. While I've highlighted the overtly rationalist components of Reid's view, such as his commitment to necessary moral truths, I've not said anything about why his view deserves to be called "intuitionist." There are, however, numerous passages that render the label apt. For example, in his discussion "Of the Sense of Duty," Reid writes, "[W]e not only have the notions of right and wrong in conduct, but perceive certain things to be right, and others to be wrong" (EAP IIII.iii.vi: 231; *cp.* V.v). Note that it is one thing to grasp that

---

[64] At EAP V.ii: 279 and V.i: 277, Reid identifies another role that affective states play. They enable agents to grasp moral concepts, which are constituents of moral judgments. In short, Reid appears to pair a sentimentalist account of concept acquisition with a non-sentimentalist understanding of motives.

an action is wrong, but it is another thing for an action to *strike* or *present itself* as being wrong. I might, for example, grasp that an action is wrong merely on the basis of testimony. But that would not imply that the act strikes me as being wrong. If it were to so strike me, then I would perceive its wrongness (in a fairly natural sense of the term "perceive"). By comparing the moral sense to external sense, Reid is keen to emphasize that just as objects present themselves as being (say) round due to the operations of external sense, so also actions strike us as being (say) wrong due to the operations of moral sense.

We could imagine scenarios in which actions strike us as wrong but we are inclined to do nothing about their wrongness. According to Reid, that is not, in fact, how we are typically so inclined. When an action strikes a plain person as (say) wrong, its wrongness also typically strikes that agent as providing decisive reasons to refrain from acting. In Reid's words, when it comes to "the right principles of conduct . . . the well disposed mind . . . feels their authority and perceives them to be genuine" (EAP III.iii.viii: 189). Plain persons, then, are often the subject of a twofold intuition in which actions strike them as being wrong and their wrongness strikes them as providing decisive reasons to act. Were plain persons to ignore these perceptions, cognitive dissonance would set in. Such a person is put at "variance with himself" (EAP III.iii.vii: 185). That a person is so affected is due to the relations that conscience bears to what I've called our motivational system. The point to underscore here is that theoretical reason does not bear these relations to the motivational system. It would be a mistake to charge Reid with failing to appreciate their differences.

Reid's first response to the Sentimentalist Objection tells us a lot about the differences between Reid's position and sentimentalism. Their differences run deep. As Reid recognized, they tend to work with fundamentally different understandings of agency, motives, and action. Because they do, it is unlikely that any single line of argument such as the Sentimentalist Objection will provide decisive reason to accept one view or the other. Instead, any case for one view or the other will have to involve a more comprehensive evaluation and critique of rival views of agency, motives, and action. This is an implication of Reid's agency-centered approach to ethical theorizing.

It would be nice if we could leave matters at this. If we could, then we would have a clear sense of how Reid would respond to the Sentimentalist Objection. But, as indicated earlier, there is another strain in Reid's thinking that is more concessive to the sentimentalist approach, as it incorporates the wide understanding of motives. This element of Reid's thinking, which figures centrally in what I am calling the second response to the Sentimentalist Objection, grants the animal motives a much more significant role to play in ethical agency and action.

Let me present three passages in which Reid's sentimentalist tendencies are apparent. The first concerns moral judgment; the second concerns judgments regarding our good on the whole; while the third concerns taste, or aesthetic judgment.

> Our moral judgments are not, like those we form in speculative matters, dry and unaffecting, but from their nature, are necessarily accompanied with affections and feelings. (EAP III.iii.vii: 180)

> I am very apt to think with Dr. Price, that, in intelligent beings, the desire of what is good, and aversion to what is ill, is necessarily connected with the intelligent nature; and that it is a contradiction to suppose such a being to have the notion of good without the desire of it, or the notion of ill without aversion to it. (EAP III.iii.ii: 156)

> Our judgment of beauty is not indeed a dry and unaffecting judgment, like that of a mathematical or metaphysical truth. By the constitution of our nature, it is accompanied with an agreeable feeling or emotion, for which we have no other name but the sense of beauty. This sense of beauty, like the perceptions of our other senses, implies not only a feeling, but an opinion of some quality in the object which occasions that feeling ... In objects that please the taste, we always judge that there is some real excellence, some superiority to those that do not please. (EIP 760)

For ease of reference, let us refer to the domains of morality, well-being, and aesthetics as normative domains. And let us make the simplifying assumption that what Reid says in these passages about judgments regarding one normative domain holds for the others. These passages appear to state three different views. According to the first passage:

(E) It belongs to the essence of normative judgments that they are affectively laden.

The second passage suggests:

(F) It is a conceptual truth that normative judgments are affectively laden.

The third (and the first) passage appears to assert:

(G) It is in virtue of the constitution of our nature that normative judgments are affectively laden.

These three views differ along two dimensions.

First, they appear to offer different proposals regarding what accounts for the intimate connection between normative judgment and affection. (E) appears to locate the affectively laden character of normative judgment in the nature of normative judgment itself. (F) does not. It appears to locate this character in the concept of normative judgment, as it indicates that it is contradictory to suppose that moral judgment fails to evoke desire. In contrast, (G) appears to locate the affectively laden character of normative judgment in neither the character of normative judgment itself nor in the concept of normative judgment, but in our human constitution.

Second, these claims differ because they appear to make different modal claims. (E) and (F) state that there is a necessary connection between normative judgment and affection. (G) does not. In fact, when Reid appeals to the constitution of our nature, he almost inevitably has in mind contingent features of our makeup due to the will of God (*cf.* IHM V.ii; EIP I.viii). If that is right, (E) and (F) entail the falsity of

> It is possible to form a normative judgment and for it not to be affectively laden.

(G) does not entail the falsity of this claim.

There seem, then, to be at least three different positions regarding the connection between normative judgment and the affections that Reid endorses. In a moment, I'll address the question of whether they can be reconciled. But let me first indicate what all three views have in common.

When Reid writes that moral judgments are necessarily connected with affection, he is not adverting to affection in some generic sense. He is instead referring to what he calls the benevolent and malevolent affections, which are animal principles of action (EAP III.ii). Reid's thought seems to be that there is a complex but integrated mental state whose components are moral judgment regarding the moral status of some particular thing and the affections. When this state involves a positive moral evaluation of something, Reid calls it "moral approbation." When it involves a negative moral assessment, he calls it "moral disapprobation" (EAP III.iii.vii).

The states that Reid calls moral approbation and disapprobation closely mirror what contemporary philosophers call "besires" or "hybrid states."[65] They possess the following features.

First, they include intentional attitudes such as compassion, gratitude, esteem, and what Reid calls "friendship." These are the affections. While the affections themselves are not feelings, they are necessarily accompanied by feelings. So when Reid writes that moral judgments are "necessarily accompanied with affections and feelings," he is simply making explicit a necessary component of the affections. Second, the affections are typically the immediate

---

[65] Altham (1986), I believe, first introduced the terminology. Little (1997) offers a defense of the philosophical respectability of besires, appealing to Hume's view as a case study.

upshot of normative judgments, produced "prior to reflection" and not by engaging in sophisticated cognitive exercises such as imagining what an impartial spectator would approve of. In this way, Reid distances his understanding of moral approbation from that offered by sentimentalists such as Adam Smith.[66] Third, the affections are *de re*/predicative attitudes. They have "persons and not things" as their immediate object (EAP III.iii.iii.: 140). In some cases, the person in question is the agent whose attitude it is (EAP III.iii.vii). Fourth, Reid repeatedly emphasizes that the affective components of the affections are grounded in normative judgments and not vice versa. Reid gestures at this commitment in the final passage quoted above when he writes that this "sense of beauty, like the perceptions of our other senses, implies not only a feeling, but an opinion of some quality in the object which occasions that feeling." In Reid's view, were you to become convinced that the object of your attitude lacks that quality (and all goes as it should), the affection would disappear.

In sum, moral approbation and disapprobation are integrated intentional states that have multiple intentional objects, as they are directed at both moral propositions and persons. They are affectively laden in the sense that they necessarily incorporate states, such as gratitude, and feelings that attend these states. While there are a variety of questions to ask about moral approbation, including why Reid believed that affection must depend on moral judgment and not vice versa, let me call attention to how much, in this second response, Reid appears to borrow from the sentimentalist tradition.

The first response we considered to the Sentimentalist Objection acknowledges that moral judgments "may" excite affections. Whether they do or not does not seem particularly central to their playing a practical role. What is central to their playing such a role is that their contents *favor* action, and agents can act in light of them. In contrast, the second response tells us that moral judgments must (in a sense of "must" yet to be determined) be connected with the affections. Moral motives are not simply that in light of which agents act. They are also what (at least partially) produce action. In this respect, they play a central role in action. This is a point emphasized by the sentimentalists.

Can the two responses to the Sentimentalist Objection that we've considered —one which is deeply at odds with sentimentalism, the other which is not—be reconciled? Perhaps.

Return to the distinction we drew in section 2 between an agent's being a pure cause of an action and being the moral cause of an action. We said that an agent is the *pure cause* of the actualization of a behavior-state B when and only when

---

[66] Reid's notes on Smith's views include comments on what he finds unsatisfactory about them; cf. MS 2131/3i/26.

she is the sole agent cause of the actualization of B. When an agent is the pure cause of the actualization of a behavior-state, then the actualization of that behavior-state is an action in the narrow sense; it is, or is the direct result of, the exertion of active power. In contrast, we said that an agent is a *moral cause* of the actualization of B when and only when she is an agent cause (though not necessarily the only agent cause) of B and can rightly be held accountable for the actualization of B. These distinctions can help make sense of why Reid appears to endorse two different responses to the Sentimentalist Objection. In the first response, Reid is concerned with agents as pure causes of action (and, so, is thinking of action in the narrow sense). In the second response, Reid is concerned with agents as not pure but moral causes of action (and, hence, is thinking of action in the wide sense).

If this suggestion is on target, it would resolve some but not all of the tensions within Reid's position. For we've seen that Reid characterizes the moral connection between moral beliefs and motivational states in different ways. In some places, he characterizes the connection as very intimate; in others, he depicts the connection as less intimate. Yet here, too, there might be a way to make sense of what Reid says.[67]

I have pointed out that, in various places, Reid seems to hold that there is a necessary connection between moral belief and motivational states. In the contemporary literature, this type of view is typically referred to as *motivational internalism*. The view is not, however, monolithic. It comes in different varieties.

One version is what I'll call *moral belief internalism*. It characterizes beliefs and affective states dispositionally. To be in these states is to be disposed to behave in certain ways. For example, under this view, to believe that murder is wrong is to be disposed to use this proposition in your theoretical and practical reasoning, to affirm that an act is wrong when you learn it is a murder, and so on. Moral belief internalism, then, affirms a necessary connection between moral beliefs (at least of a certain range) and affective states so understood. This necessary connection could be variously characterized; it might be a conceptual connection or due to the essence of moral belief. In contrast, what I'll call *moral judgment internalism* characterizes judgments and affections as the *manifestations* of beliefs and affections.[68] To judge (as opposed to believe) that murder is wrong is not merely to be disposed to behave in certain ways. It is, as it were, to have that proposition before your mind's eye. Moral judgment internalism

---

[67] Cuneo (2008) develops this proposal.

[68] In distinguishing beliefs (dispositions) from judgments (the manifestation of these dispositions), I am not employing Reid's terminology. He tends to use the terms "belief" and "judgment" interchangeably.

affirms a necessary connection between moral judgments (the manifestations of moral beliefs) and affective states. Like moral belief internalism, it could characterize this necessary connection in a variety of ways; the connection might be that of conceptual necessity or due to the essence of moral judgment.

The point to emphasize here is that moral belief internalism does not imply moral judgment internalism. Suppose that, as a matter of conceptually necessity, to believe that an act is wrong is to be in a range of motivational states, as moral belief internalism claims. Now suppose that this belief disposition is manifested on some occasion: you judge that you morally ought to act in some way. Moral belief internalism does not imply that your judgment necessarily yields some actual affective state. For different inhibitors—such as depression, fear, or injury—could conspire to block the formation of the relevant affective states. But even if these inhibitors do their inhibiting work, it would still be true that, necessarily, if you believe that you morally ought to act in some way, then you are motivated to act in that way. A parallel: suppose it is true that, necessarily, if a vase is fragile, then it will tend to break when struck. Now suppose you strike a fragile vase, but it fails to break. It does not follow that the vase is not fragile. All that follows is that something inhibited the vase's disposition to break when struck.

While I do not wish to suggest that Reid operated with this distinction between different internalist views, it does enable us to make better sense of what he says. According to the proposal, in those passages in which Reid affirms a necessary connection between moral belief and the affective states, he is articulating a version of moral belief internalism. But in those passages in which he says that the connection is due to the constitution of our nature, he is denying moral judgment internalism, recognizing that whether the actualization of a belief yields a motivational state is due (at least in part) to our constitution functioning as it should.

3.3 Conclusion

Philosophers have long held that rational intuitionist views such as Reid's are vulnerable to some telling objections. In this section, I've canvassed and addressed two fairly prominent ones. Doing so has helped us to see that the common understanding of Reid, according to which he is a rationalist intuitionist, is not wrong. But it is radically incomplete. For contrary to common depictions of rational intuitionism, Reid endeavors to tether moral reality to human nature and the human good—albeit in ways different from what one finds in the broadly Aristotelian tradition. Moreover, rather than focus entirely on the objective status of fundamental moral principles, as most rationalist positions did, Reid also concerns himself with the practical dimensions of moral judgment, offering ways of understanding the intimate relation between moral judgment and action. Under the interpretation offered, there are two rather different lines of thought in Reid regarding the connection between moral cognition and action. It is not apparent to me that they are easily reconciled. Be that as it may, positions that attempt to blend rational intuitionism, with its emphasis on the objectivity of morality, and sentimentalism, with its emphasis on motivation and action, are not common. I am hard pressed to think of another position among the moderns that does.

4 The Sidgwickean Characterization

Sidgwick begins chapter 9 of his *Methods of Ethics* by noting that his discussion has exclusively concerned the property of rightness, which implies "an authoritative prescription."[69] But, Sidgwick continues, it is possible to have organized his discussion differently. He could have organized it so that it focused on the Good, as the "Greek schools of Moral Philosophy" did.[70] This would have resulted in a discussion that focused on what is "attractive" rather than "imperative."[71] Such a discussion would require a much different approach to ethical theorizing. For it would require theorists to "throw the quasi-jural notions of modern ethics aside." Instead of asking "What is Duty and what is its ground?," as the moderns have, we'd have to ask instead "What is truly Good or the Highest Good?," as the ancients did.[72]

In her appropriation of Sidgwick's observations, Christine Korsgaard offers an explanation of this difference between the ancients and the moderns. According to Korsgaard, Plato and Aristotle saw the

> world we experience as being, in its very essence, a world of things that are trying to be much better than they are, and that really are much better than they seem . . . .In ethics, this way of viewing the world leads to what we might call the idea of excellence. . . . the endeavor to realize perfection is just the endeavor to be what you are—to be *good at being what you are*. And so the ancients thought of human virtue as a kind of excelling, of excellence.[73]

In Aristotle's thinking at least, a "well-brought up person would not need to have excellence forced upon him—as he would move naturally towards the achievement of his perfect form . . . In Greek thought, becoming excellent is as natural as growing up. We need to learn virtue; but it is as we learn language, because we are human and that is our nature."[74]

Korsgaard describes the transition from this way of thinking to that which characterizes modernity as involving a "revolution," albeit a gradual one. At the heart of this revolution is the Christian conviction that the world is not that of things striving to realize their perfection. Learning virtue is *not* natural for human beings. Rather than being naturally oriented toward excellence and being receptive to the attraction of virtue, human beings are recalcitrant matter upon which moral obligation must be imposed. In a phrase, modernity embraced an ethics of compulsion, not attraction.[75] In Korsgaard's view, it was Kant who completed the

---

[69] Sidgwick (1907, 106). Rawls (2000, 1–2) brought Sidgwick's discussion to my attention.
[70] Sidgwick (1907, 105).   [71] Sidgwick (1907, 106).   [72] Sidgwick (1907, 106).
[73] Korsgaard (1996, 3).   [74] Korsgaard (1996, 3).
[75] "Obligation differs from excellence in an important way. When we seek excellence, the force that value exerts upon us is attractive; when we are obligated, it is compulsive. For obligation is the imposition of value on a reluctant, recalcitrant, resistant matter" (Korsgaard 1996, 4).

revolution, explaining that it is human beings who impose obligation and value on ourselves and on an otherwise valueless world.[76]

Let us call the differences between antiquity and modernity to which Sidgwick points and the explanation of them that Korsgaard offers the "Sidgwickean characterization." This characterization is, I believe, illuminating, identifying deep differences in the way that the ancients and the moderns approached ethical theorizing.[77] These differences are probably not due to the fact that the ancients lacked the concepts central to modern ethical theory, such as those concerning obligation and rights. And they are probably not due to the fact that the moderns lacked or forgot about the concepts of the good for human beings or virtue.[78] Whatever the full explanation of the revolution might be, the Sidgwickean characterization is correct to suggest that the ways in which these philosophers understood these concepts and the roles they play in their thinking are deeply different.

Illuminating characterizations can, however, also distort. The Sidgwickean one is no exception, as there are prominent thinkers who don't fit the description it offers. In the modern period, sentimentalists such as Shaftesbury, Hutcheson, and Hume do not. Deontic concepts barely play a role in their ethical theorizing, while virtue (especially in the form of benevolence) does. More importantly for present purposes, Reid belongs to the class of modern philosophers that falls outside the lines of the Sidgwickean characterization. This is not because, like the sentimentalists, Reid prioritizes virtue-theoretic notions and has little to say about deontic ones, such as obligation. Quite the opposite! It is rather for two primary reasons.

First, it is because in Reid's theorizing, the concept of the human good does not recede into the background, as it did for so many of the moderns, including the sentimentalists. Instead, the notion plays a central role in Reid's agency-centered approach, being one of the two rational principles of action. Moreover, the notion of our good on the whole with which Reid works has much more in common with that employed by the ancients than with, say, the one that would be deployed in the utilitarian tradition, which is hedonistic. Reid's notion is overtly teleological, placing virtue at the heart of the human good. And yet Reid doesn't merely rehabilitate the commitments of the Aristotelian tradition. As we've seen, he rejects what he deems the tradition's problematic eudaimonistic commitments, opting (unlike the utilitarians) for a view according to which

---

[76] Korsgaard (1996, 5).

[77] It has also proven to be influential; think of Anscombe's (1958) challenge to modern moral philosophy.

[78] Although compare MacIntyre's (1984, ch. 1) "disquieting suggestion" that the modern context not only was one in which these concepts fell into disuse but also was one in which they could not be coherently understood and applied.

neither virtue nor obligation is fully grounded in our good on the whole. Virtue, in Reid's view, consists not in the actualizing of our essential capacities but in the fixed resolution to conform to one's duties and honor the rights of others.

In this regard, Reid's position is not unusual.[79] Still, his views on obligation and rights certainly do not fit the template of modern ethics with which we've become familiar. Moral obligation is not understood in terms of what maximizes the human good, per utilitarianism. Nor is it identified with a law of the will to which agents must conform in order to act, per Kant's view. Nor is it an abstract fitness relation, as Clarke and others claimed (EAP V.vii: 472).[80] Rather, moral obligations are normative relations that human agents bear to particular life-goods and persons, such as yourself and various components of your well-being. Indeed, Reid's view seems to be that for a state of, say, bodily integrity or autonomy to be a life-good is for it to be a state whose realization is such that agents have rights and obligations with respect to it.

But—and this is the second point—it should be acknowledged that the view of human beings and their good that animates Reid's position is not the one that Korsgaard identifies in her description of modern ethical theorizing. It has much more in common with the view that lies behind the sentimentalists' thinking. Rather than describe human beings as the recalcitrant material upon which obligation must be imposed and whose passions lead them in every which direction, Reid emphasizes the extent to which our affections and obligation lead us in the same direction, the former often abetting the latter. Discussing the benevolent affections, Reid writes,

> Benevolence, from its nature, composes the mind, warms the heart, enlivens the whole frame, and brightens every feature of the countenance. It may justly be said to be medicinal both to soul and body. We are bound to it by duty; we are invited to it by interest; and because both these cords are often feeble, we have natural kind affections to aid them in their operation, and supply their defects; and these affections are joined with a manly pleasure in their exertion. (EAP III.ii.iv: 121)

> All our natural desires and affections are good and necessary parts of our constitution; and passion, being only a certain degree of vehemence in these, its natural tendency is to good, and it is by accident that it leads us wrong . . . .

---

[79] See Heydt (2018, 61).

[80] "Though all vice be contrary to reason, I conceive that it would not be a proper definition of vice to say, that it is a conduct contrary to reason, because this definition would apply equally to folly . . . There are other phrases which have been used on the same side of the question, which I see no reason for adopting, such as, *acting contrary to the relations of things, contrary to the reason of things, to the fitness of things, to the truth of things, to absolute fitness* . . . The phrases . . . seem to have been invented by some authors, with a view to explain the nature of vice; but I do not think they answer that end" (EAP V.vii: 472).

> When there is no impropriety in it, much more when it is our duty, passion
> aids reason, and gives additional force to its dictates . . . . passion furnishes
> a very strong instance of the truth of the common maxim, that the corruption
> of the best things is worst. (EAP III.ii.vi: 140, 142)

Reid proceeds to detail how passions such as curiosity play a central role in theoretical inquiry, writing that "we may with justice allow no small merit to the passions, even in the discoveries and improvements of the arts and sciences" (EAP III.ii.vi: 142).

When read against the rest of the *Active Powers* and the Sidgwickean characterization of modern ethical theorizing, I find passages such as these remarkable. They are not anything that would easily flow from the pens of the most prominent figures in the sentimentalist or the rational intuitionist traditions. Obligation figures too prominently in these passages for them to be what, say, Hutcheson would write; and the passions play too central a role for them to be something that we would expect, say, Richard Price to endorse. Even Butler, to whom Reid's relatively optimistic picture of the human condition owes so much, has comparatively little to say about obligation and rights and the roles they play in agency. Like the ancients, Butler's focus is almost exclusively on virtue.

Figures such as Reid complicate a common narrative told about modern ethical theorizing that includes the Sidgwickean characterization. Like most moderns, Reid's central moral categories are those of obligation and rights. In this sense, his ethics is one of compulsion. But these deontic categories do not eclipse the role of the human good in Reid's thinking. And because they do not, Reid can be said to endorse an ethics of attraction in which (when all goes well) the passions orient us toward the human good, cooperating with our rational nature.

Perhaps the proper conclusion to draw is that the Sidgwickean characterization is correct to hold that there was indeed a conceptual revolution in ethics. But this revolution is best understood to include a variety of mini-revolutions, each having its own character. We are well familiar with those enacted by the sentimentalists, Kant, and the utilitarians. Most of us are much less familiar with Reid's. The suggestion I have developed in this book is that it is among the most intriguing of them.

References

Altham, J. E. J. 1986. "The Legacy of Emotivism." In Graham Macdonald and Crispin Wright, eds. *Fact, Science and Morality: Essays on A. J. Ayer's Language, Truth and Logic*. Oxford: Blackwell: 275–88.

Anscombe, G. E. M. 1958. "Modern Moral Philosophy." *Philosophy* 33: 1–19.

Balguy, John. 1728/1975. *The Foundation of Moral Goodness*. London: Garland.

Berker, Selim. 2019. "The Explanatory Ambitions of Moral Principles." *Noûs* 53: 904–36.

Broadie, Alexander. 2000. "The Scotist Thomas Reid." *American Catholic Philosophical Quarterly* 74: 385–407.

Butler, Bishop. 1729/2017. *Fifteen Sermons and Other Writings on Ethics*. Ed. David McNaughton. Oxford: Oxford University Press.

Chisholm, Roderick. 2003. "Human Freedom and the Self." In Gary Watson, ed. *Free Will*, 2nd ed. Oxford: Oxford University Press: 26–37.

Cuneo, Terence. 2008. "Intuitionism's Burden: Reid on Moral Motivation." *The Journal of Scottish Philosophy* 6: 21–43.

Cuneo, Terence. 2010. "Duty, Good, and God in Thomas Reid's Ethics." In Sabine Roeser, ed. *Reid on Ethics*. New York: Palgrave McMillan: 238–57.

Cuneo, Terence. 2011. "A Puzzle Regarding Reid's Theory of Motives." *British Journal for the History of Philosophy* 19: 963–81.

Cuneo, Terence. 2014. "Reid on the First Principles of Morals." *Canadian Journal of Philosophy* 41, Supplement 1: 102–21.

Cuneo, Terence, and Randall Harp. 2017. "Reid on the Autonomy of Ethics: From Active Power to Moral Nonnaturalism." *Journal of the American Philosophical Association* 2: 523–41.

Cuneo, Terence, and Randall Harp. 2019. "Reid's Regress." *Philosophical Quarterly* 69: 678–98.

Davidson, Donald. 1980. *Essays on Actions and Events*. Oxford: Oxford University Press.

Davis, William C. 2006. *Thomas Reid's Ethics*. London: Continuum.

Frankfurt, Harry. 1969. "Alternate Possibilities and Moral Responsibility." *Journal of Philosophy* 66: 829–39.

Frede, Michael. 1987. *Essays in Ancient Philosophy*. Minneapolis: University of Minnesota Press.

Haakonssen, Knud. 2007. "Introduction." In Knud Haakonssen, ed. *Thomas Reid on Practical Ethics: Lectures and Papers on Natural Religion, Self-*

government, Natural Jurisprudence and the Law of Nations. Edinburgh: Edinburgh University Press.

Harris, James. 2013. "The Government of the Passions." In James Harris, ed. *The Oxford Handbook of British Philosophy in the Eighteenth Century*. Oxford: Oxford University Press: 270–88.

Heydt, Colin. 2018. *Moral Philosophy in 18th-Century Britain*. Cambridge: Cambridge University Press.

Hume, David. 1777/1987. *Essays, Moral and Political*. Ed. Eugene Miller. Indianapolis, IN: Liberty Fund.

Hurka, Thomas. 2014. *British Ethical Theorists from Sidgwick to Ewing*. Oxford: Oxford University Press.

Kane, Robert. 2005. *A Contemporary Introduction to Free Will*. Oxford: Oxford University Press.

Korsgaard, Christine. 1996. *The Sources of Normativity*. Cambridge: Cambridge University Press.

Kroeker, Esther. 2014. "Reid's Moral Psychology: Animal Motives as Guides to Virtue." *Canadian Journal of Philosophy*, 41, Supplement 1: 122–55.

Locke, John. 1690/1975. *An Essay Concerning Human Understanding*. Ed. Peter H. Nidditch. Oxford: Oxford University Press.

Irwin, Terence. 2006. *The Development of Ethics, Vol. II*. Oxford: Oxford University Press.

Little, Margaret. 1997. "Virtue as Knowledge: Objections from the Philosophy of Mind." *Noûs* 31: 59–77.

Lowe, E. J. 2008. *Personal Agency*. Oxford: Oxford University Press.

MacIntyre, Alasdair. 1966. *A Short History of Ethics*. London: Macmillan.

MacIntyre, Alasdair. 1984. *After Virtue*, 2nd ed. Notre Dame, IN: University of Notre Dame Press.

MacIntyre, Alasdair. 1988. *Whose Justice? Which Rationality?* Notre Dame, IN: University of Notre Dame Press.

MacIntyre, Alasdair. 1990. *Three Rival Versions of Moral Inquiry*. Notre Dame, IN: University of Notre Dame Press.

Maurer, Christian. 2019. *Self-love, Egoism, and the Selfish Hypothesis*. Edinburgh: Edinburgh University Press.

Murphy, Mark. 2001. *An Essay on Divine Authority*. Ithaca, NY: Cornell University Press.

Murphy, Mark. 2011. *God and Moral Law*. Oxford: Oxford University Press

O'Connor, Timothy. 1994. "Thomas Reid on Free Agency." *Journal of the History of Philosophy* 32: 605–22.

Parfit, Derek. 2011. *On What Matters, Vol. II*. Oxford: Oxford University Press.

Poore, Gregory. 2015. "Theism, Coherence, and Justification in Thomas Reid's Epistemology." In Rebecca Copenhaver and Todd Buras, eds. *Thomas Reid on Mind, Knowledge, and Value*. Oxford: Oxford University Press: 213–31.

Radcliffe, Elizabeth S. 2018. *Hume, Passion, and Action*. Oxford: Oxford University Press.

Rawls, John. 2000. *Lectures on the History of Ethics*. Cambridge, MA: Harvard University Press.

Raz, Joseph. 1986. *The Morality of Freedom*. Oxford: Oxford University Press.

Reid, Thomas. 1785/1997. *An Inquiry into the Human Mind on the Principles of Common Sense*. Ed. Derek R. Brookes. Edinburgh: Edinburgh University Press (abbreviated as IHM).

Reid, Thomas. 1785/2002. *Essays on the Intellectual Powers of Man*. Ed. Derek R. Brookes, with annotations by Derek R. Brookes and Knud Haakonssen. Edinburgh: Edinburgh University Press (abbreviated as EIP).

Reid, Thomas. 1788/2010. *Essays on the Active Powers of Man*. Ed. Knut Haakonssen and James Harris. Edinburgh: Edinburgh University Press (abbreviated as EAP).

Reid, Thomas. 1792/2001. "On Power." *The Philosophical Quarterly* 51: 3–12 (abbreviated as OP).

Reid, Thomas. 2002. *The Correspondence of Thomas Reid*. Ed. Paul Wood. Edinburgh: Edinburgh University Press (abbreviated as Cor).

Reid, Thomas. 2007. *Thomas Reid on Practical Ethics*. Ed. Knut Haakonssen. Edinburgh: Edinburgh University Press (abbreviated as PE).

Rosen, Gideon. 2017. "Metaphysical Relations in Metaethics." In David Plunkett and Tristram McPherson, eds. *The Routledge Handbook of Metaethics*. New York: Routledge: 151–69.

Ross, W. D. 1930/2007. *The Right and the Good*. Oxford: Oxford University Press.

Rowe, William. 1991. *Thomas Reid on Freedom and Morality*. Ithaca, NY: Cornell University Press.

Schneewind, J. B. 1998. *The Invention of Autonomy*. Cambridge: Cambridge University Press.

Sehon, Scott. 2005. *Teleological Realism*. Cambridge, MA: MIT Press.

Sehon, Scott. 2016. *Free Will and Action Explanation*. Oxford: Oxford University Press.

Sidgwick, Henry. 1902. *Outlines of the History of Ethics for English Readers*. Indianapolis, IN: Hackett.

Sidgwick, Henry. 1907. *The Methods of Ethics*. Indianapolis, IN: Hackett.

Taylor, Richard. 1966. *Action and Purpose*. Englewood Cliffs, NJ: Prentice-Hall.

Turnbull, George. 1741/2008. "A Discourse upon the Nature and Origin of Moral and Civil Laws." In T. Ahnert and P. Schroder, eds. *A Methodical System of Universal Law* by George Turnbull and J. G. A. Heineccius. Indianapolis, IN: Liberty Fund.

Van Cleve, James. 2015. *Problems from Reid*. Oxford: Oxford University Press.

van Inwagen, Peter. 2017. *Thinking about Free will*. Oxford: Oxford University Press.

Van Woudenberg, René. 2004. "Thomas Reid on Memory and the Identity of Persons." In Terence Cuneo and René Van Woudenberg, eds. *The Cambridge Companion to Thomas Reid*. Cambridge: Cambridge University Press: 204–21.

Williams, Bernard. 1985. *Ethics and the Limits of Philosophy*. Cambridge, MA: Harvard University Press.

Wolf, Susan. 2015. *The Variety of Values*. Oxford: Oxford University Press.

Wolterstorff, Nicholas. 2004. "Reid on Common sense." In Terence Cuneo and René van Woudenberg, eds. *The Cambridge Companion to Thomas Reid*. Cambridge: Cambridge University Press: 77–100.

Yaffe, Gideon. 2004. *Manifest Activity*. Oxford: Oxford University Press.

Zagzebski, Linda. 2012. *Epistemic Authority*. Oxford: Oxford University Press.

Elements in Ethics

Ben Eggleston

University of Kansas

Ben Eggleston is a professor of philosophy at the University of Kansas. He is the editor of John Stuart Mill, *Utilitarianism: With Related Remarks from Mill's Other Writings* (Hackett, 2017) and a coeditor of *Moral Theory and Climate Change: Ethical Perspectives on a Warming Planet* (Routledge, 2020), *The Cambridge Companion to Utilitarianism* (Cambridge, 2014), and *John Stuart Mill and the Art of Life* (Oxford, 2011). He is also the author of numerous articles and book chapters on various topics in ethics.

Dale E. Miller

Old Dominion University, Virginia

Dale E. Miller is a professor of philosophy at Old Dominion University. He is the author of *John Stuart Mill: Moral, Social and Political Thought* (Polity, 2010) and a coeditor of *Moral Theory and Climate Change: Ethical Perspectives on a Warming Planet* (Routledge, 2020), *A Companion to Mill* (Blackwell, 2017), *The Cambridge Companion to Utilitarianism* (Cambridge, 2014), *John Stuart Mill and the Art of Life* (Oxford, 2011), and *Morality, Rules, and Consequences: A Critical Reader* (Edinburgh, 2000). He is also the editor-in-chief of *Utilitas* and the author of numerous articles and book chapters on various topics in ethics broadly construed.

About the Series

This Elements series provides an extensive overview of major figures, theories, and concepts in the field of ethics. Each entry in the series acquaints students with the main aspects of its topic while articulating the author's distinctive viewpoint in a manner that will interest researchers.

Printed in the United States
By Bookmasters